JANICE VANCLEAVE'S
Teaching the **Fun** of **Science**

to Young Learners, Grades Pre-K–2

Janice VanCleave

WILEY

John Wiley & Sons, Inc.

Published by Jossey-Bass
A Wiley Imprint
989 Market Street, San Francisco, CA 94103-1741
www.josseybass.com

Design and composition by Navta Associates, Inc.

Jossey-Bass books and products are available through most bookstores. To contact Jossey-Bass directly call our Customer Care Department within the U.S. at 800-956-7739, outside the U.S. at 317-572-3986, or fax 317-572-4002.

Jossey-Bass also publishes its books in a variety of electronic formats. Some content that appears in print may not be available in electronic books.

Library of Congress Cataloging-in-Publication Data

VanCleave, Janice Pratt.
  Janice VanCleave's teaching the fun of science to young learners, grades pre-K-2 / Janice Van-Cleave. — 1st ed.
    p. cm.
  Includes index.
  ISBN 978-0-471-47184-4 (pbk.)
  1. Science—Study and teaching (Elementary) I. Title. II. Title: Teaching the fun of science to young learners, grades pre-K-2.
  LB1585.V33 2008
    372.3'5—dc22
                                                      2007012088

Printed in the United States of America
first edition

10 9 8 7 6 5 4 3 2 1

Contents

Dedication

It is my pleasure to dedicate this book to special friends who have taught me to search for the fun of life: Stella Cathey, Sue Dunham, and Connie McLelland.

Acknowledgments

A special note of gratitude to these educators who assisted me by pretesting the activities and/or by providing innovative teaching ideas—the spring 2006 Math and Science Methods students of Beth Davidson, Lambuth University, Jackson, Tennessee: Lauren Bartholomew, Holly Turnbow, Mary Kathryn Whaley, Brandis Leverette, Michael Beasley, Amanda Saffold, Rachel Crowe, Beth Young, and Talitha Barringer.

From the Author

∙∙

The scientific activities and investigations in this book have been selected for their ability to teach the fun of science to young children, as well as to teach process skills for science inquiry. Very young children naturally love bugs, animals, and plants, and they are excited to learn about them. Young children are also curious about their bodies and want to know how they work. And though very young children may not know the words "chemistry" or "physics," just give them a bottle of soap bubbles or a magnet, and watch their eyes light up.

This book focuses on process skills because these form the foundations for scientific inquiry. The science activities and investigations in this book introduce six important process skills: observing, communicating, making and using definitions, measuring and estimating, grouping, and investigating.

The book's objective is to encourage individual and group exploration. *Exploring* is the act of searching and observing to discover information about *science*, which is a system of knowledge about the nature of things in the universe. Discovering things on their own gives kids a wonderful feeling of success. All they need is your friendly guidance, a few good ideas, and their natural curiosity.

This book is full of fun ideas. While you play and learn together, your students will find out the answers to questions such as: "Are all bugs insects?" "How does a thermometer work?" "Why do dogs pant?" "Is my foot a foot long?" "Why is my elbow wrinkled?" "What is inside a bean?" "How do wind chimes make music?" and lots of other things that children wonder about.

Guidelines for Using Science Activities and Investigations Successfully in the Classroom

Review the Teaching Tips

This book is organized into six parts: Investigating; Observing; Communicating; Making and Using Definitions; Measuring and Estimating; and Grouping. Each part opens with a brief description of the topic presented. Together these six parts comprise a total of 18 chapters with more than 100 activities and investigations.

Each chapter contains two or more activities and/or investigations, and an overview called teaching tips that provides instructions for teaching them. The overview includes the science benchmarks addressed by the activities, expectations of student learning, suggestions for preparing materials, and a mini-glossary of new terms to which students will be introduced. The overview also includes background information, interesting facts about the terms investigated as well as one or more extensions. Answers to the activities and investigations follow the extensions.

Terms introduced in each part are italicized and defined in the section's introduction, and boldfaced and defined in the teaching tips, activities, and glossary. Terms in the extensions are also in italics. All boldfaced and italic words are found in the glossary.

English and metric measurements are used throughout the book. In some activities, where precise measurements are not needed, English units, with approximate metric equivalents in parentheses, are listed. This allows the reader to use either the English or metric system but is not intended to reflect precise equivalencies between the two systems.

Get to Know the Activities

Some activities have an instruction sheet and a separate answer sheet. These activities are identified in Preparing the Materials in the teacher tips as well as on the activity sheets. The instruction sheet can be laminated and used again.

All of the activities follow a general format:

1. **Introduction:** Definitions of new terms are boldfaced and defined. Science facts needed for the activity are given.

2. **Directions:** Information on how to complete the activity.

Get to Know the Investigations

The investigations help reinforce the concepts explained in your lessons and in the activities. Read each investigation completely before starting it, and practice doing the investigation prior to class time. This increases your understanding of the topic and makes you more familiar with the procedure and the materials. If you know the investigation well, it will be easier for you to give instructions, answer questions, and expound on the topic.

Some investigations have an instruction sheet and a separate answer sheet. These investigations are identified in Preparing the Materials in the teacher tips as well as on the investigation sheets. The instruction sheet can be laminated and used again.

Investigations follow a general format (although all may not include an answer sheet):

1. **Purpose:** The goal of the investigation.

2. **Problem:** A science question to be answered by the investigation.

3. **Things to Round Up:** A list of necessary supplies (common household items) needed for each individual or group.

4. **Things to Do:** Step-by-step instructions.

5. **Data:** Collected and recorded information.

6. **Results:** A summary of the data. Generally given in the form of multiple-choice questions or fill-in-the-blank questions on the answer sheet.

7. **Conclusion:** A summary of research and experimental data; when applicable it compares the hypothesis with the experimental results. Generally given in the form of multiple-choice questions or fill-in-the-blank questions on the answer sheet.

Collect and Organize Supplies Well ahead of Time

You will be less frustrated and more successful if you have all the necessary materials for the investigations ready for instant use. Decide whether the students will be doing the investigation individually or in groups, and calculate from that how much of each material you will need for the class. I prefer to designate an area in the classroom where the supplies will be placed each time an activity or investigation is scheduled. I separate the materials and put each type of material in its own box or area on a table. I also provide boxes or trays for the students to use to carry the materials to their work areas. You may want to have your students help gather and organize supplies.

Set Up Collaborative Teams and Assign Jobs

Most investigations can be performed individually. However, forming students into teams to conduct investigations helps you manage the class and provides the best opportunity for them to learn not just the science but also how to work together. Groups of four are ideal but smaller or larger groups are also acceptable, and may in some cases be preferable. Each group works as a team to collect and analyze data, but reports may be group or individual efforts. Not only does collaboration enhance student learning, but it also reduces the number of supplies needed. Assign each group member a job or allow the group to decide who does which job. This will make group investigation time both a fun-filled adventure for the students and a time that you look forward to as one of the easiest and most organized periods of the day.

Suggested Team Job Titles and Duties

Director   This team member leads the group investigation. The director is the facilitator, but each child should do part of the investigation. The director determines what part of the work each group member performs. The director can also be the one to report to you any problems that the group may be having. One way of notifying you of the group's progress is to use 3 colored cups stacked on top of one another. The top color indicates the need of the group—red (need help immediately), yellow (when you have time we have a question), green (all is well).

Supply Manager   This team member will pick up needed supplies for the investigation from the supply table and return any unused supplies at the end of the work period. Each supply manager will need a copy of the materials list for the assignment. It helps to have all the supply managers assemble in front of the supply table at the same time so that you can identify the materials to them and give any special instructions for transporting and using the materials. The supply manager and the waste manager may be the only students allowed to move around the room.

Recorder   This team member records the observations made by the group. This can be in the form of drawings and/or written data. The recorder collects any papers that are to be turned in by the group and hands them to you. (Note: For most investigations, individual record keeping is required, so a group recorder may not always be needed.)

Waste Manager   This team member is responsible for discarding all used materials in their proper place. The waste manager should also make sure that the work area is clean and ready for the next classroom activity. The waste manager could also be the timekeeper. It is important to complete the investigation in a timely fashion so there is ample time for cleanup.

Supervise the Investigations

For very young children, read the procedures aloud, step-by-step. Students need to be encouraged to never skip or add steps to experiments. Emphasize that safety is of the utmost importance and that the instructions should be followed exactly. For some investigations, you may want to demonstrate all or part of the procedure before the students start on their own. You may stop short of showing the final step so that the students experience seeing the results for the first time themselves.

Help Students Analyze the Results of Investigations

As noted previously, it is best if you perform investigations yourself in advance so you know what to expect. Then, if the students' results are not the same as those described in the investigation, you will be better prepared to help them figure out what might have gone wrong. If something does go wrong, first go over the procedure, step-by-step, with the individual or group to make sure that no steps were left out. If all the steps were completed, try asking the students leading questions. The students can then provide their hypotheses as to why the results were not achieved. Analyze the materials. I like to ask questions such as "Does the weight of the paper affect the results?" or "Do you think temperature might make a difference?" While I prefer to brainstorm with students, sometimes I just have the group redo the investigation. This provides the opportunity to point out to students that scientists check their work to confirm their results.

Encourage Students to Report Investigation Results

Now's the time to point out that while learning science is a great individual accomplishment, it's also important to be able to communicate this knowledge through accurate understandable docu-mentation. You can assign the students individual reports or a group report to be written by the recorder with input from the whole group. Reports for investigations can range from simple drawings represent-ing the results of the investigation to a question and answer sheet which you pre-pare. Combined class results can be written on a chalkboard and used later for class dis-cussion as well as to introduce data collec-tion and organization techniques.

Make Suggestions for Further Investigations

The extension section of the teaching tips provides ideas for other studies related to the investigations. Some suggestions link the investigation to other curriculums, such as science and math.

Investigating

Investigating includes all the processes needed to ask and answer questions. These processes are called the *scientific method*. The processes are: *research* (the process of collecting information about a topic being studied), a *problem* (a science question to be solved), a *hypothesis* (an idea about the answer to a problem), an *experiment* (the process of testing in order to determine the accuracy of the hypothesis and/or to determine the answer to the problem), and a *conclusion* (a summary of the results of the investigation). Depending on what is being investigated, the order of the processes may change and some processes may not be used.

All experiments involve a *cause* and an *effect*. A *cause* is an action or act that makes something happen. An *effect* is something that happens because of an action or cause. Things in an experiment that can or do change are called *variables*. The variable that is manipulated is called the *input variable*. This results in a change in a variable called the *output variable*. Variables that are controlled so they do not change are called *controlled variables*.

Young scientists can learn to identify and use the scientific method. As they master this tool, they will be more skilled at solving questions they have about things and events in the world around them.

The Scientific Method

Benchmarks

By the end of grade 2, students should be able to
- Develop the abilities necessary to do scientific inquiry.
- Develop an understanding of the scientific method.
- Understand what constitutes evidence.
- Be able to judge the merit or strength of data used to answer questions.

In this chapter, students are expected to
- Identify a reasonable question that can be answered through investigation.
- Identify reasonable hypotheses for specific problems.
- Plan and/or conduct simple investigations.
- Use simple equipment and tools to gather data.
- Use data to identify reasonable explanations.
- Communicate investigations and explanations.

Preparing the Materials

Activity 1: Research and Problems
- Make a copy of the Research and Problems activity instruction and answer sheets for each student.

Activity 2: Problems and Hypotheses
- Make a copy of the Problems and Hypotheses activity instruction and answer sheets for each student.
- Use Extension #2 for answers about butterflies.

Activity 3: Experiment
- Make a copy of the Experiment activity sheet for each student.

Activity 4: Conclusion
- Make a copy of the Conclusion activity sheets for each student.

Investigation 1: Elbows
- Make a copy of the Elbows investigation instruction and answer sheets for each student.
- Make a flexible drinking straw available to each student.
- Students should work in pairs.

Activity 5: Investigation
- Make a copy of the Investigation activity sheet for each student.

Activity 6: Control
- Make a copy of the Control activity sheet for each student.

Investigation 2: Colored Leaves
- Make a copy of the Colored Leaves investigation instruction and data answer sheets for each student.
- On the instruction sheet, color the colored water in the glass red.
- Students should work in groups of four or more.
- Prepare identical plastic containers of red-colored water for each group. The containers should be sturdy enough so that they do not easily fall over. Tall plastic glasses or jars will work. Use the same amount of water, about 2 inches (5 cm), and drops of red food coloring for each group. Note: The water should be bright red. Use about 10 drops for each pint (500 ml) of water.
- Using the same kind of containers and amount of water, prepare a plastic container labeled "Control" for each group.
- Make two stalks of celery with leaves (preferably the pale innermost stalks) available for each group. Cut across the end of each stalk.
- FYI—For young children, a class investigation can be done. Students can make observations individually or in groups.

Presenting the Science Concepts

1. Introduce the new terms:
   chart   A way to organize data for viewing.

conclusion   A summary of information collected, including research and experiment results; a summary of the information that compares a hypothesis with experiment results.

control   A test that other tests are compared to.

data   Collected and recorded information.

experiment   A test to answer a problem; a test to check the correctness of a hypothesis.

hypothesis   An idea about what the answer to a problem is.

investigation   The process involved in asking and answering questions about science.

problem   A science question to be answered.

procedure   The instructional steps of an experiment.

purpose   The goal of an investigation.

research   The process of collecting information about a topic being studied; the act of finding information.

result   A summary of the data from an experiment.

scientific method   The steps of an investigation used in asking and answering a science question.

table   A type of chart with columns and rows.

2. Explore the new terms:

- Science investigations use all or part of the scientific method to ask and answer a science question. The scientific method is made up of five basic steps: research, problem, hypothesis, experiment, and conclusion.

- Types of investigations include describing objects, events, and organisms; classifying things; validating known facts; and doing an experiment.

- An experiment can be designed to answer a question and/or test the correctness of a hypothesis. This test does not necessarily prove that the hypothesis is right or wrong. Instead, it supports or doesn't support the hypothesis. A hypothesis may be wrong after only one test. But the test may have been done incorrectly. Thus, to prove the correctness of a hypothesis, scientists perform the same test many times. Sometimes, if variables are changed, the results change too, which may support a hypothesis that was previously considered wrong.

- While the process is called the scientific method, it can be used to ask and answer questions about topics other than science.

E X T E N S I O N

1. Fingers and elbows are not the only places on your body that have wrinkled skin and that bend. Where are other places (wrists, knees, toes, knuckles, ankles)?

2. A butterfly's long feeding tube is called a *proboscis*. When the butterfly isn't feeding, its proboscis is coiled up. When the butterfly wants to drink nectar from inside a flower, the proboscis uncoils like a party blower. Turn a party blower upside-down to show how a butterfly's proboscis coils and uncoils.

ANSWERS

Activity 1: Research and Problems
1. C
2. B
3 A
4. C

Activity 2: Problems and Hypotheses
1. C
2. B

Activity 3: Experiment
1. A

Activity 4: Conclusion
1. B
2. A

Investigation 1: Elbows
1. Stretched out

TEACHING TIPS (continued)

2. Squeezed together

3. Squeezed together

4. Stretched out

5. B and C

Activity 5: Investigation

1. B

2. B

3. A

4. B

5. B

Activity 6: Control

1. B

2. C

3. A

Investigation 2: Colored Leaves

The expected answers are listed here, but student answers may vary depending on the results of their experiment.

Hypothesis: Student answers may vary.

Colored Leaves Data Table

Start The color of the leaves on both the experiment and control celery stalks should be pale green.

Finish The color of the leaves on the experiment celery stalk should be reddish-green. The color of the leaves on the control celery stalk should not have changed. They should still be pale green.

Results:

1. T

2. F

3. F

4. T

Conclusion:

5. Student answers may vary.

6. T

© 2007 by John Wiley & Sons, Inc.

Research and Problems

The **scientific method** includes the steps of an investigation used in asking and answering a science question. Research and problems are two of the steps. **Research** is the act of finding information. One way to do research is to read. A **problem** is a science question to be answered. Doing research can answer some problems.

Directions: Read the story below. Then follow the instructions on the answer sheet.

Spiders build their webs out of strands of silk. The silk is made inside the spider's body. Spiderwebs have sticky strands. Insects that touch these sticky strands get stuck in the web. The insects try to get free by wiggling. Their wiggling makes the strands of the web move. The spider stands on the strands. When the spider feels the strands move, it runs on the strands to catch the insect.

Research and Problems

● ● ● ● ● ● ● ● ● ● ● ● ● ● ● ● ● ● ●

Directions: Read each question. Fill in the circle beside the correct answer.

1. What are spiderwebs made of?

   ○ **A.** wire

   ○ **B.** sewing thread

   ○ **C.** silk strands

2. Where does the spider make the silk for its web?

   ○ **A.** in a mixing bowl

   ○ **B.** inside its body

   ○ **C.** in the kitchen

3. What do insects do when they get stuck in a spiderweb?

   ○ **A.** wiggle to get unstuck

   ○ **B.** call 911

   ○ **C.** take a nap

4. How do spiders know an insect is stuck in their web?

   ○ **A.** They hear it calling 911

   ○ **B.** They hear it snoring

   ○ **C.** They feel the strands of the web moving

Problems and Hypotheses

Problems and hypotheses are steps in the scientific method. A problem is a science question and a **hypothesis** is an idea about what the answer to the problem is.

Directions: Read the problem. Then circle the letter for the hypothesis you think is most correct. This example is done for you.

Example: Panting

Panting is breathing quickly with your mouth open.

Problem: Why do dogs pant when it is hot?

Hypothesis:

A. When it is hot, dogs pant to cool off.

B. When it is hot, dogs pant to get rid of extra water.

C. When it is hot, dogs pant when they don't want to play.

© 2007 by John Wiley & Sons, Inc.

ACTIVITY 2
1
Answer Sheet

Problems and Hypotheses

• • • • • • • • • • • • • • • • • • • •

Directions: Read the problem. Then circle the letter for the hypothesis you think is most correct.

Nectar

Nectar is a sweet liquid in flowers.

1. Problem: How do butterflies drink nectar from flowers?

Hypothesis:

A. Butterflies stand on leaves and let the nectar from a flower petal run into their mouths.

B. Butterflies walk through nectar that is on leaves. Then they lick the liquid off their feet.

C. Butterflies have special mouth tubes that let them suck nectar out of flowers.

Staying Warm

2. Problem: How do animals stay warm in the winter?

Hypothesis:

A. Animals find warm houses to stay in during the winter.

B. Animals have coats of fur or feathers that keep them warm.

C. Animals wear coats and boots that people have thrown away.

Experiment

An experiment is one of the steps of the scientific method. An **experiment** is a test to answer a problem. An experiment has instructions, or steps, called the **procedure**. **Data** is collected and recorded information. A **result** is a summary of the data. A **chart** is one way to organize data for viewing

Directions: Read the procedure steps for the experiment and study the data. Then circle the letter for the correct result.

Procedure:

1. Observe Figure A in the Balancing Data Chart. Notice that the figure does not lean.

2. Like Figure A, stand with your feet about 12 inches (30 cm) apart and your hands to your sides.

3. Notice that your body does not lean.

4. Observe Figure B in the Balance Data Chart. Notice the direction that the figure leans.

5. Like Figure B, balance on your right foot by lifting your left foot.

6. Notice the direction that your body leans.

Results:

A. To balance on your right foot, you must lean your body toward the right.

B. To balance on your right foot, you must lean your body toward the left.

C. To balance on your right foot, you do not have to lean your body.

Balancing Data Chart

A.

B.

Conclusion

A conclusion is a step in the scientific method. A **conclusion** is a summary of the information collected, including research and experiment results.

Directions: Read the story, the experiment, and its result. Then circle the letter of the best conclusion.

1. Evaporation

Evaporation is the change of a liquid to a gas. It takes energy for a liquid to evaporate. When water evaporates from a surface, the water absorbs energy from the surface. This causes the surface to cool off.

You sweat when you get hot. When sweat evaporates from your skin, your skin cools off.

Experiment: Wet your arm with water, then blow across the wet area on your arm.

Result: Your arm feels cooler.

Conclusion:

A. When water evaporates from your skin, it causes the skin to feel cooler. This means that evaporation of sweat is one of the ways your body has of keeping your body warm.

B. When water evaporates from your skin, it causes the skin to feel cooler. This means that evaporation of sweat is one of the ways your body has of keeping your body cool.

C. When water evaporates from your skin, it causes the skin to feel cooler. This means that evaporation of sweat doesn't change your body temperature.

Conclusion (continued)

Directions: Read the story, the experiment, and its result. Then circle the letter of the best conclusion.

2. Thermometer

A **thermometer** is an instrument that measures temperature. When the liquid line in a thermometer goes up, it indicates an increase in temperature. When the line goes down, it indicates a decrease in temperature.

Experiment: Stand one thermometer in a cup of warm water. Stand a second thermometer in a cup of cold water.

Results: The liquid line of the thermometer in the warm water went up. The liquid line of the thermometer in the cold water went down.

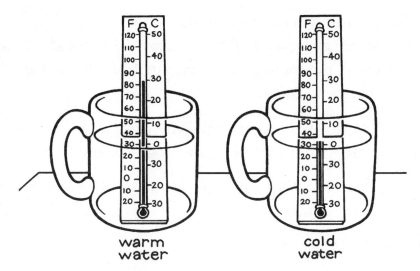

warm water   cold water

Conclusion:

A. The liquid line of the thermometer went down in cold water and up in warm water. This means the temperature of the warm water was higher than the temperature of the cold water.

B. The liquid line of the thermometer went down in cold water and up in warm water. This means the thermometers are not accurate.

C. The liquid line of the thermometer went down in cold water and up in warm water. This means that thermometers cannot be used to measure how hot or cold water is.

Elbows

● ● ● ● ● ● ● ● ● ● ● ● ● ● ● ● ● ● ●

Purpose: To determine why elbows are wrinkly.

Problem: Why are elbows wrinkly?

Round Up These Things

1 flexible drinking straw
1 partner

Things to Do

1. Try to bend the straw where it is not wrinkled. It is difficult to bend and may break.

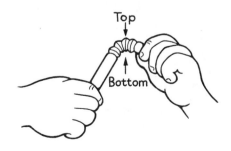

2. Try to bend the straw where it is wrinkled. Look at the top and bottom of the wrinkles. In the Wrinkled Skin Data table, check the column that completes statements 1 and 2. A **table** is a type of chart with columns and rows.

Top

Bottom

3. Ask a friend to hold his or her arm straight up. Look at the skin on your friend's elbow. Then, in the data table, check the column that completes statement 3.

4. Ask your friend to bend his or her elbow. Look at the skin on your friend's elbow. Then, in the data table, check the column that completes statement 4.

INVESTIGATION 1
Answer Sheet
1

Elbows

● ●

Wrinkled Skin Data		
Statements	Stretched Out	Squeezed Together
1. The wrinkles on top of the straw are		
2. The wrinkles on the bottom of the straw are		
3. When the elbow is straight, the skin covering it is		
4. When the elbow is bent, the skin covering it is		

Directions: Read the sentences that follow and fill in the circle beside the two sentences that should be part of the conclusion for the experiment.

5. ◯ **A.** The straw easily bends where there are no wrinkles.

◯ **B.** The wrinkled skin on the elbow stretches out when the elbow bends.

◯ **C.** Wrinkles keep your skin from breaking when your elbow bends.

ACTIVITY 5
Instruction Sheet
1

Investigation

Investigations use the scientific method to ask science questions and to discover their answers. The **purpose** is the goal of an investigation.

Directions: Read the story. Then follow the instructions on the answer sheet.

Phoebe wondered how butterflies drink. She guessed that they stand on a leaf and let the water on a flower petal run into their mouths. Phoebe read about butterflies. She discovered that they have a **proboscis**, a long mouth tube they drink through. This tube works much like a drinking straw. Instead of drinking water from flowers, butterflies drink nectar, which is a sweet liquid food.

Investigation

● ● ● ● ● ● ● ● ● ● ● ● ● ● ● ● ● ● ●

© 2007 by John Wiley & Sons, Inc.

Directions: Identify the parts of the scientific method in the story. Fill in the circle beside the correct answers.

1. The purpose of Phoebe's investigation:

   ○ **A.** To find out how butterflies fly.

   ○ **B.** To find out how butterflies drink.

2. The science problem:

   ○ **A.** How do butterflies fly?

   ○ **B.** How do butterflies drink?

3. Phoebe's hypothesis:

   ○ **A.** Butterflies stand on leaves and let water from a flower petal run into their mouths.

   ○ **B.** Butterflies do not drink. Instead, they hold their heads up and catch raindrops.

4. How Phoebe checked the correctness of her hypothesis:

   ○ **A.** Testing butterflies.

   ○ **B.** Reading about butterflies.

5. The conclusion:

   ○ **A.** Butterflies have sponges that soak up liquids.

   ○ **B.** Butterflies do not let water run into their mouths. They drink through special strawlike mouth tubes.

ACTIVITY 6

Instruction Sheet

1

Control

Some investigations have a control. A **control** is a test that other tests are compared to.

Directions: Read the story. Then follow the instructions on the answer sheet.

Lacey put six white carnations in a vase of water. She wondered if the cut flowers would turn bright red if she put food coloring in the water. She guessed that the more coloring she added to the water the redder the petals would be. But Lacey wanted to know for sure. So she decided to experiment to find out. She filled six identical containers with equal amounts of water. In five of the containers, she put a different number of drops of red food coloring. She labeled each container with the number of drops of added food coloring. Then she stood a cut flower in the water of each container. To tell how much the petal colors changed, Lacey wanted one of the flowers to stay white. So she did not put any color in the water for this flower.

Control

• •

1. Read the following questions. Fill in the circle beside the sentence that tells the problem for Lacey's investigation.

   ○ **A.** How does the type of container affect the color of the petals of cut flowers standing in water inside the container?

   ○ **B.** How does the amount of coloring in water affect the color of the petals of cut flowers standing in the water?

   ○ **C.** How does the amount of water affect the color of the petals of cut flowers standing in the water?

2. Read the following statements. Fill in the circle beside the sentence that tells Lacey's hypothesis.

   ○ **A.** As the amount of red coloring in the water increases, the color of the flower petals will be a lighter red.

   ○ **B.** As the amount of red coloring in the water decreases, the color of the flower petals will be a darker red.

   ○ **C.** As the amount of red coloring in the water increases, the color of the flower petals will be a darker red.

3. Read the following statements. Fill in the circle beside the sentence that tells the control that Lacey used.

   ○ **A.** A white carnation was placed in water with no coloring added.

   ○ **B.** All the containers were identical with the same amount of water.

   ○ **C.** The same kind of flowers was used for each test.

Colored Leaves

Purpose: To make a hypothesis and conduct an experiment to see if the hypothesis is correct.

Problem: Will red dye in water move through a plant and color its leaves?

Hypothesis: (Before starting the experiment, circle your answer on the Colored Leaves answer sheet.)

Round Up These Things

crayons
2 stalks of celery
1 glass of red-colored water
1 glass of water marked "control"

Things to Do

1. On the answer sheet, color the colored water in the glass red.

2. Stand one of the celery stalks in the glass of red-colored water so that the cut end is underwater.

colored
water

3. Stand the second celery stalk in the glass of water without coloring. This will be the control.

control

clear
water

4. Observe the color of the leaves on the celery stalk in the glass of colored water. Then color the leaves on the drawing in the Colored Leaves Data table marked "Start" to match the color of the leaves.

5. Repeat step 3, observing the color of the leaves of the control.

6. After 5 or more days, again observe the color of the leaves on the celery stalks. Then color the leaves on the drawings in the data table marked "Finish."

7. Follow the instructions on the Colored Leaves answer sheet.

ACTIVITY 1

1

Answer Sheet

Colored Leaves

● ● ● ● ● ● ● ● ● ● ● ● ● ● ● ● ●

Directions: Follow the instructions for each part.

Hypothesis: Circle the answer that completes your guess.

Red dye in water will:

    A. not move through a plant and color its leaves.

    B. move through a plant and color its leaves.

Colored Leaves Data

Start	Finish
colored water clear water (Control)	colored water clear water (Control)

ACTIVITY 1

1

Answer Sheet

Colored Leaves (continued)

● ● ● ● ● ● ● ● ● ● ● ● ● ● ● ● ● ● ● ●

Results: Write a T in the blank if the sentence is true. Write an F in the blank if the sentence is false.

1. _____ The pale green leaves on the celery stalk standing in red-colored water changed to a reddish-green color.

2. _____ The pale-green leaves on the celery stalk standing in red-colored water remained pale green in color.

3. _____ The pale-green leaves on the control celery stalk changed to a reddish-green color.

4. _____ The pale-green leaves on the control celery stalk remained pale green in color.

Conclusion: Write a T in the blank if the sentence is true. Write an F in the blank if the sentence is false.

5. _____ The experiment supported my hypothesis.

6. _____ If a cut end of a stalk of celery is placed in red-colored water, the red color in the water moves up the stalk to the leaves. The pale-green leaves change to a reddish-green color. This takes about 5 days.

Cause and Effect

Benchmarks

By the end of grade 2, students should be able to
- Identify cause and effect if given choices.
- Identify variables if given choices.

In this chapter, students are expected to
- Identify cause and effect.
- Identify input, output, and controlled variables.

Preparing the Materials

Activity 1: Cause and Effect
- Make a copy of the Cause and Effect activity instruction and answer sheets for each student.

Investigation 1: Height Changes
- Make a copy of the Height Changes investigation sheet for each student.
- This is a homework assignment.
- Compare students' results.

Activity 2: Variables
- Make a copy of the Variables activity instruction and answer sheets for each student.

Activity 3: Controlled Variables
- Make a copy of the Controlled Variables activity instruction and answer sheets for each student.

Presenting the Science Concepts

1. Introduce the new terms:

   cause   An action or an act that makes something happen.

   controlled variable   A variable that is kept the same.

   effect   Something that happens because of a cause.

   input variable   A variable that you change.

   output variable   A variable that changes because of the input variable.

   variable   Something that can be changed or can change on its own.

2. Explore the new terms:
   - Variables are things that if changed might affect the results of an experiment. For example, if you want to determine how fertilizer affects plant growth, you would use different amounts of fertilizer on different plants of the same type and measure their growth. Fertilizer is the input variable (the cause) and plant growth is the output variable (the effect).
   - The fertilizer test would not be valid if different kinds of plants or different kinds of fertilizer were used or if the plants received different amounts of light or water. These are the variables that have to be controlled.

EXTENSION

- Students can investigate how the position of the Sun affects the direction of their own shadows.
- Students can investigate how the type of paper affects the paper's ability to curl.

ANSWERS

Activity 1: Cause and Effect

Cause: B   Effect: D

Activity 2: Variables

1. Input variable: B   2. Input variable: A
   Output variable: A   Output variable: B

Activity 3: Controlled Variables

1. Input variable: B
   Output variable: C
   Controlled variable: A

2. Student answers will vary. Possible answers include the amount of water and the type of container.

Cause and Effect

● ● ● ● ● ● ● ● ● ● ● ● ● ● ● ● ● ● ● ●

A **cause** is an action or an act that makes something happen. An **effect** is something that happens because of an action or cause.

Directions: Read the story. Then read the cause choices and circle the letter of the correct cause. Read the effect choices and circle the letter of the correct effect. This example is done for you.

Example: Shadows

Rachel noticed that during the day, the position of the Sun changes. Sometimes the Sun is low in the sky and sometimes it is high in the sky. She also observed that when the Sun changes position, the length of her shadow changes.

Cause

A. Change in the bright-
ness of the Sun

B. Change in the
position of the
Sun

Effect

C. Change in the length
of Rachel's shadow

D. Change in Rachel's
height

ACTIVITY 1

2

Answer Sheet

Cause and Effect

• •

Directions: Read the story. Then read the cause choices and circle the letter of the correct cause. Read the effect choices and circle the letter of the correct effect.

Curls

As part of a craft project, Sara pressed a strip of paper against the edge of a table. Keeping the paper taut, she pulled down on the paper, sliding the entire strip across the table edge. Rubbing the paper against the table made it flatter on one side, so it curled up.

Cause

A. Cutting paper to make it smaller

B. Rubbing paper to make it flatter on one side

Effect

C. Straightens paper

D. Curls paper

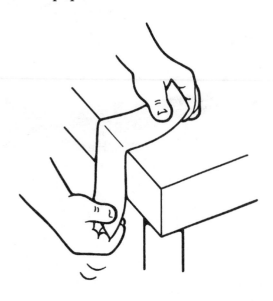

Height Changes

Directions: Read the story.

Jared read that a person is shorter at the end of the day than in the morning. This is because when standing or sitting, gravity pulls the ends of the bones of the back together and the person becomes shorter. **Gravity** is a force that pulls things down. During the night, while lying down, gravity pulls the sides of the bones down, but the ends are not pulled together. This lets the bones separate slightly and the person becomes taller.

Cause: Change in the way gravity pulls on the bones

Effect: Change in height

Directions: Ask an adult to measure your height in the late afternoon and again the next morning.

Height in the afternoon _____

Height in the morning _____

Were you shorter in the morning? _____

Variables

A **variable** is something that can change. In an experiment, the part that you cause to change is called the **input variable**. The effect of changes in the input variable is due to changes in something called the **output variable**.

Directions: Read the story. Then read the input variable choices and circle the letter of the correct input variable. Read the output variable choices and circle the letter of the correct output variable. This example is done for you.

Example: Pupil changes

Weston read that the dark spot in the center of your eye is called the **pupil**. The pupil is a hole in your eye that can change size depending on the brightness of the light. The pupil gets larger in bright light and smaller when the light is dim. Weston decided to do an experiment to find out how much light is needed to make the pupil change size. What are the variables of his experiment?

Input variable

(A.) amount of light

B. size of the pupil

Output variable

A. amount of light

(B.) size of the pupil

Variables

Directions: Read the two stories. Then read the input variable choices and circle the letter of the correct input variable. Read the output variable choices and circle the letter of the correct output variable.

Tree Shade

1. Easton observed that some trees make more shade than do other trees. He wondered if the size of the trees' leaves caused this. Easton decided to measure the size of tree leaves to find out if trees with big leaves make more shade. What are the variables of his experiment?

Input variable

A. amount of shade

B. size of the leaves

Output variable

A. amount of shade

B. size of the leaves

Flight Path

2. Conner noticed that when he released an inflated balloon, the balloon flew in a zigzag path. He decided to experiment to find out if the shape of the balloon would change the shape of the balloon's flight path. What are the variables of his experiment?

Input variable

A. balloon shape

B. shape of flight path

Output variable

A. balloon shape

B. shape of flight path

Controlled Variables

Variables are things that can change. An experiment should have one input variable and one output variable. But an experiment can have many controlled variables. **Controlled variables** are variables that you keep from changing so they do not affect the results of your experiment.

Directions: Read the story. Then follow the instructions. This example is done for you.

Example: Paper Chains

Chloë wanted to make paper chain necklaces. She wondered if the width of the paper strips would affect the length of the necklace. Chloë decided to do an experiment to find out how the widths of the strips changed the length of the necklace.

What are the variables in Chloë's experiment? Circle the letter of the correct variable for each variable type.

Input variable	Output variable	Controlled variable
A. length of strips	**A.** length of strips	**(A.)** length of strips
(B.) width of strips	**B.** width of strips	**B.** width of strips
C. length of necklace	**(C.)** length of necklace	**C.** length of necklace

List two other controlled variables for Chloë's experiment.

• color of paper

• type of paper

© 2007 by John Wiley & Sons, Inc.

Controlled Variables

● ● ● ● ● ● ● ● ● ● ● ● ● ● ● ● ● ●

Directions: Read the story. Then follow the instructions.

Light Seekers

Robin noticed that the leaves on one of her plants were bending toward a window. She wondered about this and read about plants. Robin discovered that plants grow so that they get more light. She decided to experiment to find out how long it takes for the leaves on her plant to bend toward the light.

1. What are the variables in Robin's experiment? Circle the letter of the correct variable for each variable type.

Input variable

A. type of plant

B. length of time

C. position of leaves

Output variable

A. type of plant

B. length of time

C. position of leaves

Controlled variable

A. type of plant

B. length of time

C. position of leaves

2. List two other controlled variables for Janet's experiment.

● _____

● _____

Observing

Observing is the act of examining something by using your senses. *Senses* are the specialized functions an organism has of knowing what is going on around it. Kids come pre-equipped with five observing tools, which are their five senses: sight, touch, hearing, smell, and taste. As they learn and grow, their ability to apply these tools effectively in learning about their environment improves.

Sight

Benchmarks

By the end of grade 2, students should be able to
- Realize that organisms use their senses to interact with their environment.
- Recognize that living things have features that help them to survive.
- Use the science process skill of vision.
- Recognize that living things are made up of smaller parts.
- Recognize that smaller parts of living things contribute to the operation and well-being of entire organisms.

In this chapter, students are expected to
- Make visual observations.
- Recognize that animals have different kinds of eyes.
- Identify adjectives that can be used to describe the physical appearance of something.
- Determine the difference between facts and opinions.
- Make a model of an insect.
- Observe the smaller parts of an insect and identify their functions.

Preparing the Materials

Activity 1: Using Your Eyes
- Make a copy of the Using Your Eyes activity sheet for each student.

Activity 2: Describing Words
- Make a copy of the Describing Words activity sheet for each student.
- Make sure each student has crayons or markers.

Activity 3: Fact or Opinion?
- Make a copy of the Fact or Opinion? activity sheet for each student.

Activity 4: Models
- Make a copy of the Models activity instruction and answer sheets for each student.

Investigation 1: Insect Model
- Make a copy of the Insect Model investigation instruction and answer sheets for each group of four or more students.
- For each group cut twelve 3-inch (7.5-cm) pieces of chenille craft stems (available at craft stores) in half, then cut each piece in half again. Three craft stems will make 12 pieces.
- Prepare 4 wings for each group. Prepare them by tracing wing shapes on tissue paper and cutting them out. Tape one of the 3-inch (7.5-cm) craft stems to each wing as shown.
- Form 3 balls from the clay: 1 small (red), 1 medium (blue), and 1 large (yellow).

Activity 5: Animal Eyes
- Make a copy of the Animal Eyes activity instruction and answer sheets for each student.

Presenting the Science Concepts

1. Introduce the new terms:

   adjective A word that describes something.

   brain The part of your body that receives and decodes nerve messages so you know how things feel. It is located in your head.

   fact Something that is true.

   model Something that is made to represent an object or thing.

   nerve A tiny threadlike fiber that sends coded messages to your brain.

   observing The act of examining something by using your senses.

   opinion A belief that someone has about something.

   senses What an organism uses to know and feel what is going on around it.

   sight One of your senses. You need your eyes to see.

2. Explore the new terms:
- Observing is one of the most important parts

of being a scientist. But equally important is being able to describe accurately what you observe. Students need to know the difference between adjectives that are facts or opinions. Scientific observations must always be factual.

- There are five senses: sight, touch, hearing, smell, and taste. Only the sense of sight will be studied in this chapter.

- Each of the senses send coded messages to the brain. The brain decodes the messages so you know how things look, feel, sound, smell, or taste.

- Insects have three body parts.

- Point out that although Bugsy the Insect in Activity 4 doesn't have wings, most insects have two or four wings. Insects' wings are always attached to the middle body part, the **thorax**.

- Examples of models include diagrams and physical representations.

- Spiders have two body parts and four pairs of legs. Spiders are not insects. So not all creepy-crawlies are insects.

EXTENSION

Students can color the picture of the mother and daughter on the Using Your Eyes activity sheet. Use the colored picture to evaluate students' abilities to make visual observations. Do this by preparing an activity sheet with directions such as the following:

Directions:

Observe the picture you colored. Now, color the circle next to the object with the color that matches the object in your picture.

1. Jennifer's hair ◯
2. Makinzie's hair bow ◯
3. Makinzie's watch ◯
4. Makinzie's shirt ◯

ANSWERS

Activity 1: Using Your Eyes
1. Jennifer
2. Makinzie
3. Makinzie
4. Jennifer
5. Jennifer
6. Makinzie
7. Makinzie
8. Jennifer
9. Makinzie
10. Jennifer

Activity 2: Describing Words
Students should have colored the pictures labeled A, C, and D.

Activity 3: Fact or Opinion?
1. F
2. O
3. O
4. F
5. F

Activity 4: Models
1. three
2. head
3. thorax
4. abdomen
5. six
6. three
7. three, three

Investigation 1: Insect Model
1. an insect
2. six
3. three
4. six, three
5. thorax

Activity 5: Animal Eyes
1. chameleon
2. cat
3. eagle
4. eagle
5. cat

Using Your Eyes

3

You **observe** things with your **senses**. Tiny threadlike fibers called **nerves** send coded messages from your senses to your **brain**. Your brain decodes these messages so you know what is going on around you. **Sight** is one of your senses. You observe with your eyes by looking at things. You use your eyes to observe things such as color, size, and shape.

Directions: Look at the picture of Makinzie and Jennifer. Then draw a line from each statement to the person it describes. The first one is done for you as an example.

1. Has on long pants.
2. Is wearing a watch.
3. Has shoelaces.
4. Is wearing glasses.
5. Has on earrings.
6. Has a bow in her hair.
7. Has the shortest hair.
8. Is exercising.
9. Pants have a pattern.
10. Has one knee bent.

Makinzie

Jennifer

ACTIVITY 2

3 Describing Words

When you observe something, you tell what you see using "describing words." Words that describe things are called **adjectives**.

Directions: Observe each picture. In the sentence above each picture an adjective (describing word) is underlined. If the adjective for a picture is correct, color the picture.

Example: The dog has a <u>long</u> tongue.

A. The <u>big</u> elephant is being weighed.

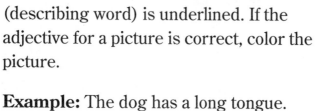

B. Krista is wearing a <u>tiny</u> necklace.

C. The Sun is <u>bright</u>.

D. Tyler's crown has <u>eight</u> jewels.

ACTIVITY 3

3 Fact or Opinion?

In making scientific observations, it is important to use facts and not opinions. A **fact** is something that is true and that can be proven. An **opinion** is a belief that someone has about something and that cannot be proven.

Example:

   Fact: The horse has four legs.

   Opinion: The horse is pretty.

Directions: Look at the picture of Vicki and the shoe salesman. Then read each statement. Write F next to each fact and O next to each opinion.

_____ **1.** Vicki is holding a monkey.

_____ **2.** The monkey is cute.

_____ **3.** The man likes children.

_____ **4.** The man is measuring Vicki's foot.

_____ **5.** The man has bigger feet than Vicki.

Models

A **model** is something that is made to represent an object or a thing. Diagrams are one example of a model. Models are made in order to make something easier to see. Models of small things, such as insects, are made larger so that the insect parts can be studied.

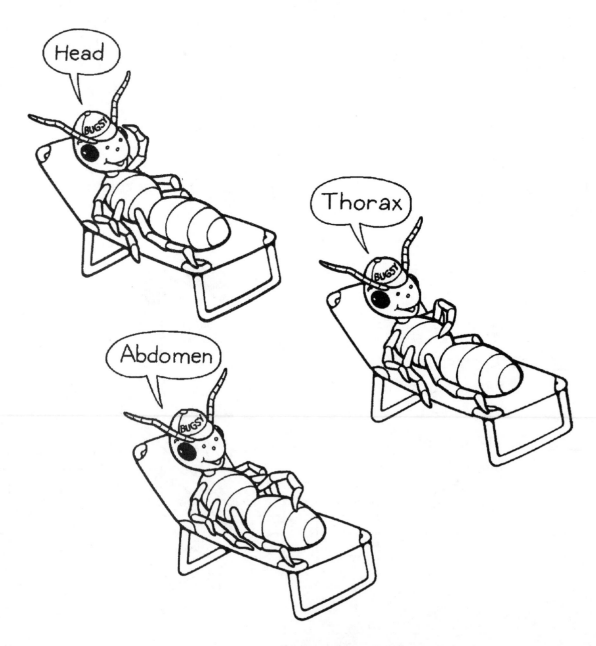

ACTIVITY 4

3

Answer Sheet

Models

● ● ● ● ● ● ● ● ● ● ● ● ● ● ● ● ● ● ● ●

Directions: Look at the three pictures of Bugsy, the cartoon insect. Bugsy is pointing to different parts of his body with his legs. Touch the body parts and say their names with Bugsy. Then circle the word that correctly completes each sentence.

1. Bugsy has _____ body parts.

one   two   three

2. The end body part with eyes is called the _____.

head   thorax   abdomen

3. The legs are connected to the body part called the _____.

head   thorax   abdomen

4. The end body part opposite the head is called the _____.

head   thorax   abdomen

Directions: Touch each of Bugsy's legs as you count them. Then circle the word that correctly completes each sentence.

5. Bugsy has _____ legs.

four   six   eight

6. Bugsy has _____ pairs of legs.

one   two   three

7. The 3 + 3 rule helps to identify insects. This rule means that insects have _____ body parts and _____ pairs of legs.

one   two   three   one   two   three

Insect Model

● ● ● ● ● ● ● ● ● ● ● ● ● ● ● ● ● ● ● ●

Purpose: To make a model of basic insect parts.

Round Up These Things

2 small paper clips
3 balls of clay: red, blue, and yellow
eight 3-inch (7.5-cm) craft stems
4 wings
2 wiggle eyes

Things to Do

1. Stick a paper clip into the red and yellow balls of clay.

2. Push the three balls of clay together, with the medium-size blue ball in the center. The small ball of clay will be the insect's head, the middle ball the thorax, and the large ball the abdomen.

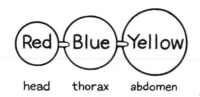

head   thorax   abdomen

3. Use 6 of the craft stems to form the insect's legs. Stick 3 legs in each side of the thorax. Bend each leg as shown.

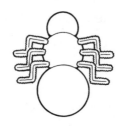

4. Stick 2 wings on each side of the insect's thorax above the legs by pushing the end of each craft stem into the clay. The front wings should cover part of the hind wings.

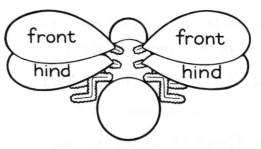

front   front
hind   hind

5. Press the 2 wiggle eyes into each side of the head.

6. Use the remaining 2 craft stems to make antennae. Push them slightly into the head between the eyes. Bend the ends of the stems as shown.

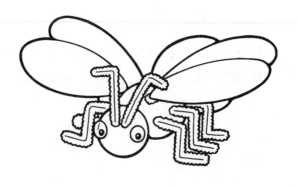

Insect Model

● ● ● ● ● ● ● ● ● ● ● ● ● ● ● ● ● ● ● ●

Directions: Circle the word that correctly completes each sentence.

Results:

1. The model made represents _____.

  an insect   a spider

2. The model has _____ legs.

  four   six   eight

3. The model has _____ body parts.

  one   two   three

Conclusion:

4. Insects have _____ legs and _____ body parts.

  two   four   six   one   two   three

5. Most insects have wings that are connected to the _____.

  head   thorax   abdomen

Animal Eyes

Directions: Read the stories. Follow the instructions on the answer sheet.

Chameleons

Chameleons have two eyes that stick out from their heads. Each eye works by itself, so this animal can see forward and backward at the same time without moving its head. Chameleons are **predators**, which means they eat other animals. The animals they eat are called **prey**.

Eagles

Eagles can see eight times better than a person who has good eyesight. These birds can see a rabbit that is one mile away. Eagles need good eyesight so they can find prey while flying above the ground.

Cats

Cats' eyes seem to glow when you shine a light at them. But their eyes really do not glow. Instead, there is a mirrorlike surface inside a cat's eye that reflects the light. This surface works much like the reflectors on road signs or on a bicycle, and it helps cats to see at night when there is very little light.

ACTIVITY 5

3

Answer Sheet

Animal Eyes

● ● ● ● ● ● ● ● ● ● ● ● ● ●

Directions: After reading about animal eyes, circle the correct animal each sentence describes.

1. This animal can see forward and backward at the same time.

    eagle   chameleon

2. If you shine a light on them, the eyes of this animal seem to glow.

    chameleon   cat

3. This animal can see a rabbit that is a mile away.

    cat   eagle

4. This animal can see eight times better than a person who has good vision.

    eagle   chameleon

5. Inside the eyes of this animal is a mirror-like surface that reflects light.

    chameleon   cat

Hearing

Benchmarks

By the end of grade 2, students should be able to
- Realize that organisms use their senses to interact with their environment.
- Recognize that living things have features that help them to survive in different environments.
- Use the science process skill of hearing.
- Recognize that living things are made up of smaller parts.
- Recognize that smaller parts of living things contribute to the operation and well-being of entire organisms.

In this chapter, students are expected to
- Identify the part of the body that collects sounds.
- Describe how the size of an animal's ears helps protect it from enemies.
- Explain what makes sound.
- Recognize high and low sounds.
- Identify the sounds that different things make.
- Explain how people make sounds when they talk or hum.

Preparing the Materials

Activity 1: Hearing
- Make a copy of the Hearing activity instruction and answer sheets for each student.

Activity 2 : Animal Ears
- Make a copy of the Animal Ears activity sheet for each student.
- Make one green and one red crayon available for each student.

Investigation 1: Musical Cans
- Make a copy of the Musical Cans investigation instruction and answer sheets for each student.

- Have empty metal cans without any paper covering available for each group. (Soup cans work well.)
- Students need to work in groups of two or more.
- Make one plastic bottle filled with tap water available for each group. (Water bottles work well.)

Activity 3: Loudness
- Make a copy of the Loudness activity instruction and answer sheets for each student.

Investigation 2: Squealer
- Make a copy of the Squealer investigation instruction and answer sheets for each student.
- Have one 9-inch (23-cm) round balloon available for each student.

Presenting the Science Concepts

1. Introduce the new terms:

   decibel (dB)   The unit used to measure the loudness of sound.

   hearing   One of your senses. You hear with your ears.

   outer ear   The part of the ear you can see that collects sounds and directs them inside the ear.

   pitch   How high or how low a sound is.

   sound   Energy produced by vibrating objects.

   symbol   Something that stands for or represents something else; letters or figures that represent words.

   vibrate   To shake or move back and forth.

   vocal cords   Two small rubber band–like flaps in your throat that vibrate when air from the lungs passes through them.

2. Explore the new terms:

   - Most animals have two outer ears.
   - The outer ears of different kinds of animals vary in size and shape.

- The outer ears of people and many animals are shaped so that they can collect sounds.
- The loudest animal sound is made by the blue whale. The sound is measured at 188 dB.
- Thunder is one of nature's loud sounds, which vary with distance. It can be 120 dB or more. Other common sounds and their loudness are: whispering (20 dB), leaves rustling (30 dB), heavy rainfall (50 dB), and shouting in someone's ear (110 dB).
- Examples of symbols using letters to represent a word are: dB for decibel, in for inch, hr for hour, yr for year, m for meter, and L for liter.
- The voices of people are different because of the differences in their vocal cords, as well as differences in things like the shape and size of their mouth, tongue, and lips. You shape sounds produced by your vibrating vocal cords into words with your tongue and lips.

EXTENSION

People often have difficulty determining the direction from which a sound is coming if it is in front or in back of their head. It is easier for them to determine the direction if the sound is on one side or the other where their ear is. To demonstrate this, arrange the students so that they are sitting in a circle. Blindfold one student and have him or her stand in the center of the circle. The objective is for one student to clap his or her hands, then the blindfolded child must determine the direction of the sound. One way to do this is to tell students to clap only when you point to them. The blindfolded child can then turn and point in the direction he or she thinks the sound came from. Give each guesser three turns. Make sure the sounds come from the front, back, or side of the child.

Answers

Activity 1: Hearing
1. C
2. E
3. A
4. D
5. F
6. B

Activity 2: Animal Ears
1. Fact (green)
2. Opinion (red)
3. Fact (green)
4. Fact (green)
5. Opinion (red)
6. Fact (green)

Investigation 1: Musical Cans
1. lower
2. can
3. lower
4. lower
5. slower

Activity 3: Loudness
1. 95 dB
2. 120 dB
3. 180 dB

Investigation 2: Squealer
1. B
2. B
3. vibrate
4. vibrate
5. vibrate

Hearing

Hearing is one of your senses. You hear sound with your ears. **Pitch** is how high or how low a sound is. **Sounds** are made when something vibrates. **Vibrate** means to shake or move back and forth. The slower an object vibrates, the lower is the pitch of the sound. The faster the vibration, the higher the pitch. As an object vibrates, it causes the air around it to vibrate. This vibrating air is collected by your **outer ear** (the part of the ear you can see) and directed inside your ear. From inside the ear, special parts send messages to your brain. Your brain has stored information about the sounds you have heard.

Directions: Each picture on this sheet is of an object making a sound that you have heard before. Look at each picture. Then draw a line from each written sound to the picture it matches. This example is done for you.

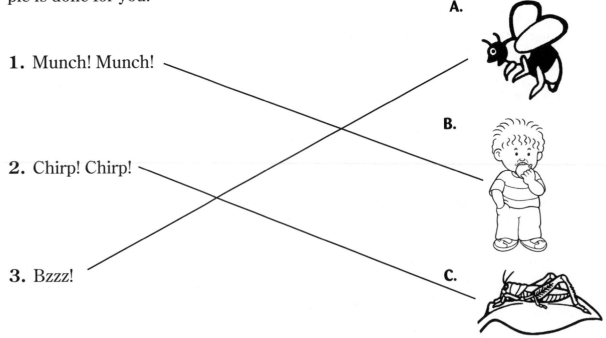

1. Munch! Munch!

A.

2. Chirp! Chirp!

B.

3. Bzzz!

C.

ACTIVITY 1
4
Answer Sheet

Hearing

Directions: Each picture on this sheet is of an object making a sound that you have heard before. Look at each picture. Then draw a line from each written sound to the picture it matches.

A.

B.

1. Achoo

C.

2. Tweet

3. Brrrrrrrrrrrrrring

D.

4. Lub-dub

5. Meow

E.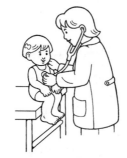

6. Arf

F.

ACTIVITY 2

4 Animal Ears

Most animals have outer ears. Some animals have big ears and some have small ears. Big ears catch more sound than do small ears. Elephant ears are very large. Because their ears are so big, elephants hear very well. Elephants also cool off their bodies by flapping their ears.

A polar bear has small ears. Polar bears hear about as well as people do. A polar bear needs small ears so it can swim fast. Large ears would catch on the water and slow it down. With small ears, the polar bear can also flatten them against its head and keep water out of them.

Directions: After reading about animal ears, decide if each statement is a fact or an opinion. Color the square green for fact and red for opinion.

- [ ] 1. Polar bears have small ears.

- [ ] 2. Elephants have cute ears.

- [ ] 3. Elephants hear well because their large ears catch a lot of sounds.

- [ ] 4. When polar bears flatten their ears in the water, it helps them to swim faster.

- [ ] 5. It is fun to watch an elephant flap its ears.

- [ ] 6. When a polar bear flattens its ears while swimming, water doesn't get into them.

INVESTIGATION 1

Instruction Sheet

4

Musical Cans

● ● ● ● ● ● ● ● ● ● ● ● ● ● ● ● ● ● ● ●

Purpose: To show how vibration speed changes the pitch of sound.

Round Up These Things

1 metal can
1 unsharpened pencil
1 plastic bottle of water

Things to Do

1. Stand the can on a table.

2. Use the pencil to gently tap on the side of the empty can near its rim.

3. Continue to tap against the can as a helper slowly pours the water from the bottle into the can. Observe the sound made as the water rises in the can.

4. Tap the can and look for any movement in the surface of the water.

5. Follow the instructions on the answer sheet.

INVESTIGATION 1

Answer Sheet

4

Musical Cans

● ● ● ● ● ● ● ● ● ● ● ● ● ● ● ● ● ● ●

Directions: Circle the word that correctly completes each sentence.

Data:

1. As the water rises in the can, the sound gets _____.

lower   higher

2. When the can is tapped, you _____ see the water vibrate.

can   cannot

Results:

3. As water is added to the can, the pitch of the sound gets _____.

lower   higher

Conclusion:

4. Pitch is how high or low a sound is. The slower an object vibrates, the lower is its pitch. As the amount of water in the can increases, the _____ is the pitch when the can is tapped.

higher   lower

5. The more water in the can, the _____ the can vibrates when it is tapped.

faster   slower

Loudness

● ●

Scientists measure the loudness of sounds in **decibels**. Instead of writing out words for measurements, scientists sometimes use **symbols**, which are letters that represent a word. The symbol for decibel is **dB**.

Directions: Each path of the maze starts with one of the pictures below. Follow the paths on the Loudness answer sheet to find out the loudness in decibels of each of the objects in the pictures. Write the answers in the blanks below each object's name.

1. Hair dryer on high speed

2. Thunder

3. Space rocket taking off from launch pad

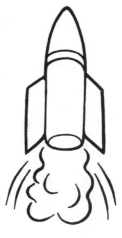

ACTIVITY 3
4
Answer Sheet

Loudness

• • • • • • • • • • • • • • • • • • • •

1. hair dryer   2. thunder   3. rocket
____db   ____db   ____db

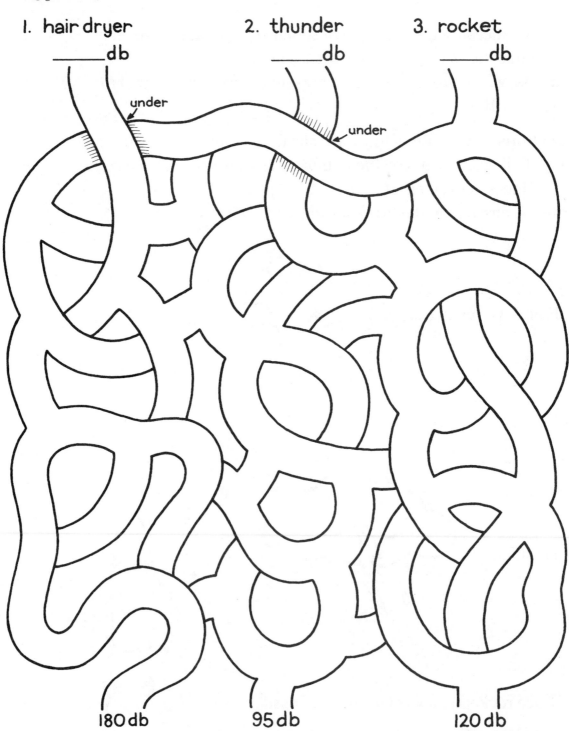

under

under

180 db   95 db   120 db

Squealer

• •

Purpose: To show how people make sounds.

Round Up These Things

one 9-inch (23-cm) round balloon

Things to Do

1. Inflate the balloon and hold the opening closed with your fingers.

2. Hold the neck of the balloon with your fingers on each side and stretch the rubber outward to let out a little air at a time.

3. Follow the instructions on the Squealer answer sheet.

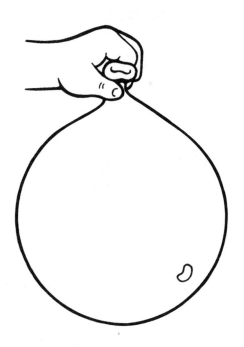

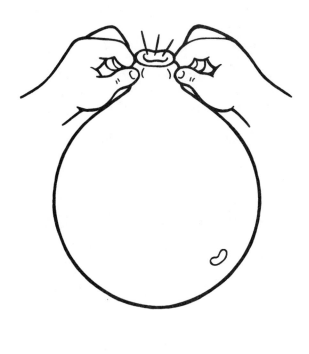

Squealer

● ● ● ● ● ● ● ● ● ● ● ● ● ● ● ● ● ●

Directions: Circle the letter in front of the statement that correctly completes each sentence.

Data:

1. As the air leaves the balloon,

    A. no sound is heard.

    B. a squealing sound is heard.

    C. a sound like a whisper is heard.

Results:

2. When air passes through the stretched rubber of the balloon,

    A. no sound is heard.

    B. a squealing sound is heard.

    C. a sound like a whisper is heard.

Directions: Circle the word that correctly completes each sentence.

Conclusion:

3. Something must _____ to make a sound.

    vibrate   stiffen

4. Air passing through the stretched rubber of the balloon causes the rubber to _____.

    vibrate   stiffen

5. When you talk, air from your lungs passes through two small rubber band–like flaps in your throat called **vocal cords**. Your vocal cords must _____ to make a sound.

    vibrate   stiffen

Smell

Benchmarks

By the end of grade 2, students should be able to
- Realize that organisms use their senses to interact with their environment.
- Recognize that living things have features that help them to survive.
- Use the science process skill of smell.
- Recognize that living things are made up of smaller parts.
- Recognize that smaller parts of living things contribute to the operation and well-being of entire organisms.

In this chapter, students are expected to
- Use their sense of smell to make observations.
- Understand that the smell of a flower attracts some insects.
- Determine how animals interact with their environment through their senses.
- Recognize specific differences among plants of the same kind.
- Recognize that when substances combine they may retain their individual properties (e.g., oil and rubbing alcohol).

Preparing the Materials

Activity 1: Smelling Words
- Make a copy of the Smelling Words activity sheet for each student.
- Make crayons available for students.

Activity 2: Scent
- Make a copy of the two Scent activity sheets for each student.
- Students should work in groups of two to four.
- Make two or more flower petals available for each student. Use one kind and color of flower for the entire class. (Check with a local florist for discarded flowers that have a nice scent, such as roses.)

- Make crayons available that match the color of the flower petals.
- Make one moist towelette available for each student.
- Make one plastic jar available for the class. Crushed flower petals will be collected in the jar.
- After the activity is completed, make "flower perfume" by adding rubbing alcohol to the jar of flower petals. Put the jar in a place where it will not be disturbed but a place where students can observe it. Encourage them to notice any changes in the appearance of the contents of the jar, such as the color of the liquid. Generally, the color of the flowers changes the liquid's color, but it may not change much. **CAUTION: Alcohol is flammable. Keep it away from heaters or open flames.**

Investigation 1: Flower Perfume
- Make one copy of the Flower Perfume investigation sheet for each student.
- Label the jar of crushed petals and rubbing alcohol "flower perfume."
- Prepare one cotton swab moistened with "flower perfume" for each child.

Presenting the Science Concepts

1. Introduce the new terms:

   nose   The part of the body that identifies smells.

   odor   Also called smell or scent.

   scent   A certain smell.

   smell   A sense that identifies scents; the scent itself.

2. Explore the new terms:
   - Smell happens inside your nose. Odors dissolved in the air you breathe pass through your nose and stimulate special cells at the top of the nasal cavity. These cells send a message to the brain, which identifies the smell.

- Your sense of smell is 10,000 times more sensitive than your sense of taste.

- You never forget a smell. Once your nose has detected the odor of fish, you will always recognize it when you smell it.

- The oil in many sweet-smelling flowers serves multiple purposes. It is used in making perfume, and it also attracts insects, which transfer pollen from one flower to another.

EXTENSION

How is the sense of smell related to the sense of taste? Students can determine why food has little taste when they have a cold. When blindfolded and holding their nose, students will have difficulty identifying the taste of different kinds of juice. This is because most of what is thought to be taste is actually a smell. Without the sense of smell, foods basically taste salty, sweet, bitter, or sour or a combination of these.

Answers

Activity 1: Smelling Words

Across	Down
3. odor	**1.** evaporation
4. scent	**2.** nose
	4. smell

Activity 2: Scent: Part I

1. sweet
2. soothing
3. strong (may be mild depending on flowers)

Activity 2: Scent: Part II

1. warm
2. heats
3. heated
4. gas
5. nose

Investigation 1: Flower Perfume

Flower Data: The expected answers are sweet, soothing, or mild, but student answers may vary.

1. oil
2. oil

ACTIVITY 1

5 Smelling Words

Directions: Choose the word that matches each clue and write the answers in the puzzle. Then color the picture.

evaporation
odor
nose
smell
scent

Across

3. Also called smell or scent.

4. A certain smell.

Down

1. The changing of a liquid into a gas.

2. The part of your body that identifies smells.

4. A sense that identifies odors.

ACTIVITY 2

5

Scent: Part I

Flowers smell sweet because of oils in their petals. These oils **evaporate**, which means they change from a liquid into a gas. You smell the oils when this gas enters your nose.

Directions: Follow the steps of the experiment.

1. Look at the color of the flower petals.

2. Draw one of the petals in the box.

3. Color your drawing the same color as the flower's petal.

4. Tear the flower petals into small pieces.

5. Place the petal pieces in your hand, then rub your hands together to crush the petals.

6. Smell the crushed petals in your hand.

7. Place the crushed petals in a jar, then clean your hands.

Directions: Circle one of the words in each row that describes the smell of the crushed flower petals.

Results:

1. sweet   sour

2. soothing   hurtful

3. mild   strong

Petal

© 2007 by John Wiley & Sons, Inc.

Scent: Part II

Directions: Follow the steps of the experiment. Then circle the word that correctly completes the sentence.

- Press the palms of your hands together.
- Quickly rub your hands back and forth a few times.

Result:

1. Rubbing your hands together makes them feel _____ .

     warm   cold

Directions: Circle the word that correctly completes each sentence.

2. Rubbing your hands together crushes and _____ the petals.

     heats   cools

3. When the oil in the petals is _____ , it evaporates faster.

     heated   cooled

4. When the oil in the petals evaporates, it changes to a _____ .

     gas   liquid

5. You smell the oils in the petals when the gas enters your _____ .

     eyes   nose

INVESTIGATION 1

5 Flower Perfume

Purpose: To demonstrate one way to make flower perfume.

Round Up These Things

1 cotton swab moistened with liquid from the flower petal jar that has been soaking for seven days.

Things to Do

1. Rub the cotton swab on your wrist. **CAUTION: Keep the swab away from your eyes, nose, and mouth.**

2. Allow the liquid to dry. Then smell your wrist.

3. In the Flower Data table, circle one of the words in each row that describes the smell of the crushed flower petals.

Flower Data	
1. sweet	sour
2. soothing	hurtful
3. mild	strong

Directions: Read the conclusion. Then circle the word that correctly completes each sentence.

Conclusion: The oils in the flower petals mixed with the rubbing alcohol. When you dabbed the liquid on your skin, at first you smelled the rubbing alcohol. When your arm dried, the alcohol was gone, but the sweet-smelling oils from the flower petals were left on your skin. This is because alcohol evaporates quickly. Oils evaporate slowly. As they evaporate, you smell their sweet scent.

1. The liquid is a mixture of rubbing alcohol and _____ from flower petals.

   oil   water

2. The part of the liquid mixture that smells like flowers is the _____.

   alcohol   oil

Taste

Benchmarks

By the end of grade 2, students should be able to
- Realize that organisms use their senses to interact with their environment.
- Recognize that living things have features that help them to survive.
- Use the science process skill of taste.
- Recognize that living things are made up of smaller parts.
- Recognize that smaller parts of living things contribute to the operation and well-being of entire organisms.

In this chapter, students are expected to
- Make taste observations.
- Recognize that the sense of smell helps the sense of taste.
- Identify adjectives that can be used to describe tastes.
- Identify the parts of the tongue where different tastes are sensed.

Preparing the Materials

Activity 1: Taste Buds
- Make a copy of the Taste Buds activity sheet for each student.

Investigation 1: Tasty
- Make a copy of the Tasty investigation instruction and answer sheets for each student.
- Prepare a testing plate for each student. Draw two lines to divide a paper plate into four even parts. Label the parts: sugar, salt, cocoa, and lemonade. In the labeled parts, place about ¼ teaspoon (0.62 mL) of each of the following: sugar, salt, unsweetened cocoa, and lemonade powder.
- For each student, prepare two 5-ounce (150-mL) paper cups about half-full with tap water.
- Students should not share testing plates or cotton swabs. You may wish to have a special testing area(s) where students do the investigation one at a time.

- Have a waste can available for students to discard their testing plate, cotton swabs, and empty cups. Note: A large coffee can makes a good container for liquid waste, such as water. You can later empty the can down the sink.

Investigation 2: Added Flavor
- Make a copy of the Added Flavor investigation instruction and answer sheets for each student or group.
- Students should work in pairs. To help control students from drinking after one another, have one pair of students at a time in the testing area.
- To prevent students from identifying the juices by color or labels on a container, pour the juices into an unlabeled pitcher or jar. Cover the container with paper or add food coloring to the juices so they are not their original color.
- Each student will need three 3-ounce (90-mL) paper cups. Two of the cups will have different kinds of fruit juice, such as grape, apple, orange, cranberry, or pineapple. Students need only enough juice to make two taste tests. The third cup will be filled with tap water. Make two sets of testing cups. In set one, label the juice "Cup 1" and "Cup 2." Label the second set the same way. This will allow you to use the same instruction and answer sheets for each student. Make the juices in set one different from set two. Color the juices different colors to help in keeping them separate.
- Prepare the cups in advance, and pass them out to students in the testing areas after the testers have been blindfolded. The first group of testers will receive set one cups. The second group of testers will receive set two cups after they are blindfolded.
- Each student needs his or her own blindfold. This can be cloth cut long enough to tie around the students' heads, or tape a strip of adding machine tape around their heads to cover their eyes.
- Make available liquid waste and solid waste disposal containers.
- After the first group of testers has completed the investigation, the partners switch roles.

You may wish to do this either immediately or after a class discussion about the investigation.

Activity 2: Taste Words
- Make a copy of the Taste Words activity sheet for each student.
- Make a green crayon available for each student.

Presenting the Science Concepts

1. Introduce the new terms:

   flavor   How things taste.

   saliva   The liquid in your mouth that softens food.

   taste   A sense that identifies flavors. You need taste buds to taste.

   taste buds   Groups of cells in your mouth and throat that let you taste things that are sweet, salty, bitter, and sour.

   tongue   A part of the body used for tasting.

2. Explore the new terms:
   - Saliva also helps digest food. Digestion is the process of breaking food into small parts that the body can use.
   - The bumps on your tongue are called papillae (say: puh-PIH-lee), and most of them contain taste buds.
   - Most taste buds have very sensitive microscopic hairs that send messages to the brain about how something tastes.
   - Most people have about 10,000 taste buds, and they're replaced about every two weeks.
   - As people get older some of the taste buds that die are not replaced. An older person may only have 5,000 working taste buds. That's why certain foods may taste stronger to you than they do to older adults.
   - Smoking, at any age, can reduce the number of working taste buds a person has.
   - About 25 percent of people are super tasters. This means that they have a greater sensitivity to different tastes than most people. This is because they have inherited the characteristic of having more taste buds.

EXTENSION

In some people, temperature alone can cause the perception of taste. For example, warming the tip of the tongue may produce a sweet sensation, while cooling it gives a salty or sour sensation. For each student, make an ice cube using distilled water, and place a craft stick in it. Tell students only that different solutions have been frozen and they will identify the taste as being sweet, sour, salty, or bitter. The student to be tested will be blindfolded. Ask the student to stick out his or her tongue, then, holding an ice cube by the craft stick, touch the tip of the student's tongue with the ice cube. Students should write their answer down instead of saying it aloud. After each student has been tested, take a survey of how many tasted each of the four tastes. Used ice cubes can be placed in a container. After they melt, the water can be poured in the sink and the sticks discarded in the trash.

Answers

Activity 1: Taste Buds

1. D
2. B
3. C
4. A

Investigation 1: Tasty

1. sweet
2. salty
3. bitter
4. sour
5. Four
6. saliva
7. bitter

Investigation 2: Added Flavor

2. The answer should be yes as smell helps identify flavors.

Activity 2: Taste Words

The order of the words on the path is: taste, tongue, mouth, taste buds, flavor, sour, sweet, salty, and bitter.

Taste Buds

Taste is a sense that identifies flavors. Your **tongue** is a part of your body used for tasting. **Taste buds** are groups of cells in your mouth and throat that identify the flavor of the food you eat. **Flavor** is how things taste. The liquid in your mouth, called **saliva**, mixes with the food and makes a liquid that can enter the taste buds. There are some taste buds in other parts of your mouth and throat, but most are on your tongue. The four common flavors are sweet, sour, salty, and bitter. Usually, some areas of the tongue are better at identifying certain tastes than others. Sweet is identified best near the front, sour along each side, salty is on each side near the tip, and bitter is in the back.

Directions: In the drawing, a shape indicates where the four tastes are best identified. Match each shape to its taste. Then write the letter for the taste next to the number it matches.

A. sweet

B. sour

C. salty

D. bitter

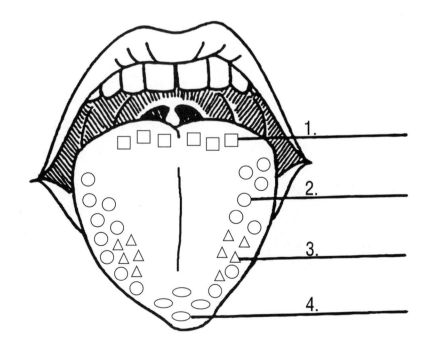

© 2007 by John Wiley & Sons, Inc.

Tasty

Purpose: To determine how the four basic flavors taste.

Round Up These Things

1 sheet of paper towel
4 cotton swabs
two 5-ounce (30-mL) paper cups of water
1 taste-testing plate with sections for sugar, salt, cocoa, and lemonade powder

Things to Do

1. Lay the paper towel on a table. Place the cotton swabs on the towel.

2. Dip one cotton swab in one of the cups of water.

3. Touch the wet cotton swab to the sugar in the plate.

4. Lick the swab with your tongue, then throw the swab in the trash.

5. Drink some water from the second cup, to wash out the taste of the food. This will be your drinking cup.

6. Record your observations on the Tasty answer sheet.

7. Repeat steps 2 through 6 to test the salt.

8. Repeat steps 2 through 6 to test the cocoa.

9. Repeat steps 2 through 6 to test the lemonade powder.

Tasty

● ● ● ● ● ● ● ● ● ● ● ● ● ● ● ● ● ● ● ●

Directions: Circle the word that correctly completes each sentence.

Data:

1. Sugar tastes _____.

    sweet   sour   salty   bitter

2. Salt tastes _____.

    sweet   sour   salty   bitter

3. Cocoa tastes _____.

    sweet   sour   salty   bitter

4. Lemonade tastes _____.

    sweet   sour   salty   bitter

Results:

5. _____ different flavors were tasted.

    Two   Three   Four

Conclusion:

6. Food mixes with _____ in your mouth so it can enter the taste buds.

    soda   saliva

7. Taste buds let you taste things that are sweet, sour, salty, and _____.

    bitter   cold   hot

Added Flavor: Part I

● ● ● ● ● ● ● ● ● ● ● ● ● ● ● ● ● ● ●

Purpose: To identify juices using only taste.

Round Up These Things

two 3-ounce (90-mL) paper cups
    containing different types of fruit
    juice, labeled "Cup 1" and "Cup 2"
one 3-ounce (90-mL) cup of tap
    water
1 blindfold
3 crayons: red, blue, and green
1 partner

Things to Do

1. Blindfold your partner so he or she cannot identify the juices by sight. Your partner is doing a taste test and is called the tester.

2. Instruct the tester to pinch his or her nose closed during the entire experiment. It is important not to sneak a smell during the experiment, so the juices are not identified by smell.

3. Hand Cup 1 to the tester and give him or her instructions to drink some of the juice and identify it.

On the tester's answer sheet, use the red crayon to circle the name of the juice in Juice List 1 that the tester identifies.

water

4. After making the identification, have the tester drink some water to wash out the taste of the juice.

5. Hand Cup 2 to the tester and give him or her instructions to drink the juice and identify it. On the tester's answer sheet, use the red crayon to circle the name of the juice in Juice List 2 that the tester identifies.

INVESTIGATION 2

6

Instruction Sheet

Added Flavor: Part II

Purpose: To show that smell makes things taste different.

Round Up These Things

two 3-ounce (90-mL) paper cups containing different types of fruit juice, labeled "Cup 1" and "Cup 2"
one 3-ounce (90-mL) cup of tap water
1 blindfold
3 crayons: red, blue, and green
1 partner

Things to Do

1. Instruct the tester to keep the blindfold on but to release his or her nose.

2. Hand Cup 1 to the tester and give him or her instructions to drink some of the juice and identify it. On the tester's answer sheet, use the blue crayon to circle the name of the juice in Juice List 1 that the tester identifies.

3. After making the identification, have the tester drink some water to wash out the taste of the juice.

4. Hand Cup 2 to the tester and give him or her instructions to drink the juice and identify it. On the tester's answer sheet, use the blue crayon to circle the name of the juice in Juice List 2 that the tester identifies.

5. Take the blindfold off of the tester's eyes.

6. Using the green crayon, circle the juice in Juice List 1 and 2 that your teacher says is correct.

7. Return the answer sheet to the tester.

8. Complete the results on your answer sheet.

© 2007 by John Wiley & Sons, Inc.

Added Flavor

Data:

Part I: Taste

Juice List 1 (Cup 1)

orange   pineapple   grape   apple
cranberry   other

Juice List 1 (Cup 2)

orange   pineapple   grape   apple   cranberry   other

Part II: Taste and Smell

Juice List 2 (Cup 1)

orange   pineapple   grape   apple   cranberry   other

Juice List 2 (Cup 2)

orange   pineapple   grape   apple   cranberry   other

Directions: Write the answers in the blanks.

Results:

1. How many juices did you identify correctly? _____

2. Did smell help you identify the juices? _____

NAME ______________________________

ACTIVITY 2 6

Taste Words

Help Kevin find the path to David and the picnic.

Directions: Read the word in each space. If the word is a taste word, color the space green. Do not color the other spaces.

ear
tongue
taste
mouth
eye
toes
nose
hand
taste buds
flavor
sour
sweet
hair
salty
skin
bitter
JUICE

Touch

Benchmarks

By the end of grade 2, students should be able to
- Realize that organisms use their senses to interact with their environment.
- Recognize that living things have features that help them to survive.
- Use the science process skill of touch.
- Recognize that living things are made up of smaller parts.
- Recognize that smaller parts of living things contribute to the operation and well-being of entire organisms.

In this chapter, students are expected to
- Make touch observations.
- Identify adjectives that can be used to describe touch senses.
- Identify their type of fingerprints.
- Determine how animals use touch to interact with their environment.

Preparing the Materials

Activity 1: Touch Words
- Make one copy of the Touch Words activity instruction and answer sheets for each student.

Investigation 1: Painless
- Make one copy of the Painless investigation instruction and answer sheets for each student.
- Because a child's hair is to be cut, it is suggested that this investigation be a homework assignment, or get a parent's permission to cut the end of one strand of hair.

Investigation 2: Touchy
- Make one copy of the Touchy investigation answer sheet for each student and one instruction sheet for each pair of students.
- Students need to work in pairs.

- Collect class results and make a graph to reveal how many students have each type of fingerprint pattern.

Activity 2: Where Am I?
- Make one copy of the Where Am I? activity sheet for each student.
- Make crayons available for each student.

Investigation 3: Ridged
- Make one copy of the Ridged investigation answer sheet for each student and one investigation sheet for each group of students.
- Make a penny, transparent tape, and a magnifying lens available to each student or group of students.

Presenting the Science Concepts

1. Introduce the new terms:

   fingerprint   The ridges on your fingertip that make up a special pattern.

   pressure   A touch sense that lets you know that something is pushing on your body.

   skin   The outer protective covering on your body.

   touch   One of the body's five senses.

2. Explore the new terms:
   - The four common touch sensations are hot, cold, pain, and pressure.
   - Pain is an important sensation. If you did not feel pain, you could touch hot surfaces and burn yourself or touch sharp objects and cut yourself without knowing you were being burned or cut.
   - We become unaware of some pressure touches. For example, we do not notice the pressure of the air on our bodies, but we do notice wind, which is moving air. We feel clothes when we first put them on, but then we are not aware of them unless they are uncomfortable.

© 2007 by John Wiley & Sons, Inc.

TEACHING TIPS (continued)

- Like hair, it doesn't hurt to cut fingernails or toenails because the part that is not attached to the body is dead.
- Identical twins have the same fingerprint pattern. Their prints are very similar, but there are small differences

EXTENSION

- Prepare mystery touch bags by gluing different items, such as popcorn, cotton, sand, fake fur, and wax paper onto index cards. Number the bags and place one card in each bag. Students are to reach into the bag and touch the textured surface of the card. They should have examples of all the touch cards in order to compare their touch sensation with what they see.
- Using the touch cards, have students determine the opposite sensation for each card. Provide a word list of antonyms describing touch sensations that are opposite from each other. For example, soft, hard and rough, smooth.

  Students can discover that ridges on their fingertips make it easier to pick up things. They can do this by following these steps:

  1. Place a penny on a table.
  2. With their thumb and index (pointing) finger, the students should try to pick up the penny.
  3. Students should cover the ends of their thumb and index finger on one of their hands with the tape.

4. Students should attempt to pick up the penny with their taped fingers.

Answers

Activity 1: Touch Words
1. touch
2. nerves
3. brain
4. pressure
5. skin

Investigation 1: Painless
1. No
2. Yes
3. A, D
4. B, D

Investigation 2: Touchy
1. Yes
2. No
3. A, C
4. A, C

Activity 2: Where Am I?
Picture at the beach.

Investigation 3: Ridged
1. Student answers will vary.
2. C

Touch Words

Touch is one of your body's five senses. Unlike all the other senses, your sense of touch is located all over your body. This is because your sense of touch comes from nerves in your skin. **Skin** is the outer protective covering on your body. Nerves are tiny threadlike fibers that send coded messages to your brain. Your brain is in your head. It is the control center that receives and decodes nerve messages so you know how things feel. Four common touch messages sent by nerves are hot, cold, pain, and pressure. **Pressure** is when something pushes on your body. For example, you are aware of the pressure of a heavy book bag.

Directions: Polly the Parrot can talk. On the Touch Words answer sheet, fix the mistakes that Polly has made. The incorrect word is underlined in each sentence. Choose a word from the word list below to replace it. Write the word in the blank space.

My name is Polly.

Word List

skin

nerves

pressure

brain

touch

Touch Words

● ● ● ● ● ● ● ● ● ● ● ● ● ● ● ● ● ● ● ●

Polly says:

1. Your sense of <u>smell</u> is located all over your body.

_____

_____

2. Your sense of touch comes from <u>oil</u> in your skin.

_____

_____

3. Nerves send coded messages to your <u>ears</u>.

_____

_____

4. <u>Cold</u> is the feeling when something pushes on your body.

_____

_____

5. <u>Hair</u> is the outer protective covering of your body.

_____

_____

Painless

Purpose: To show that hair that is not attached to the body is dead.

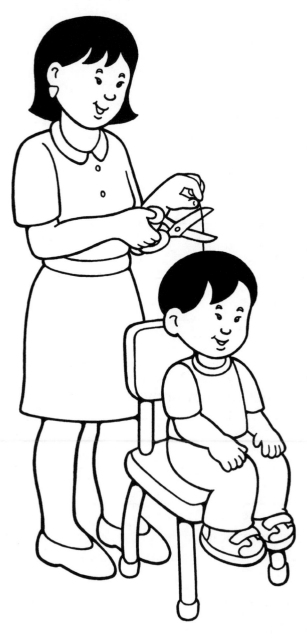

Round Up These Things

yourself
scissors

Things to Do

1. **Adult step:** Loosely hold one strand of hair on the child's head.

2. **Adult step:** Notify the child when you are ready to cut the end of the hair, then use the scissors to cut the end of the hair.

3. With your fingers, hold several strands of hair close to your scalp. Gently pull your hair upward. Do not pull hard enough to pull the hair out.

4. Follow the instructions on the Painless answer sheet.

Painless

Directions: Circle the word that answers each question.

Data:

1. Did it hurt when your hair was cut?   Yes   No

2. Did it hurt when you pulled your hair?   Yes   No

Directions: Circle the letters in front of the two sentences that describe the results of this experiment.

Results:

3. **A.** It does not hurt to cut your hair.

   B. It hurts to cut your hair.

   C. It does not hurt to pull your hair.

   D. It hurts to pull your hair.

Directions: Circle the letters in front of the two sentences that are correct.

Conclusion:

4. **A.** It hurts to pull your hair because the part of the hair attached to the body is dead.

   B. It hurts to pull your hair because the part of the hair attached to the body is alive.

   C. It doesn't hurt to cut your hair because the part of the hair attached to the body is dead.

   D. It doesn't hurt to cut your hair because the part of the hair not attached to the body is dead.

INVESTIGATION 2
Instruction Sheet
7

Touchy

Purpose: To determine if hair is alive.

Round Up These Things

yourself
1 partner

Things to Do

1. Sit in a chair with your arm resting on a table.

2. Turn your head away and close your eyes while your partner very gently moves one finger back and forth against the ends of the hairs on your arm.

3. Change place with your partner and repeat steps 1 and 2.

4. Follow the instructions on the Touchy answer sheet.

Touchy

● ● ● ● ● ● ● ● ● ● ● ● ● ● ● ● ● ●

Directions: Circle the word that answers each question.

Data:

1. Could you feel it when the hair on your arm was touched?

   Yes   No

2. Did it hurt when the hair on your arm was touched?

   Yes   No

Directions: Circle the letters in front of the two sentences that describe the results of this experiment.

Results:

3. **A.** It does not hurt when the hair on my arm was touched.

   B. It hurt when the hair on my arm was touched.

   C. It did not hurt, but I could feel it when the hair on my arm was touched.

Directions: Circle the letters in front of the two sentences that are correct.

Conclusion:

4. **A.** The hair growing out of my arm is not alive, but the part of the hair beneath the skin is alive.

   B. The hair growing out of my arm is alive, but the part of the hair beneath the skin is dead.

   C. When a hair is touched, the part of the hair beneath the skin moves. That is why I could tell when a hair was touched.

   D. When a hair is touched, only the part of the hair not attached to the skin moves. That is why I could not tell when a hair was touched.

ACTIVITY 2

7

Where Am I?

Directions: Read about Tina. Then color the picture that describes where Tina is.

Tina loves the cool wet feel of water on her skin. She likes boats. The Sun makes Tina's skin feel hot. She plans to rest and drink a can of cold juice before walking in the dry soft sand that gives way with each step. She needs to collect shells for her science project. Many shells are found near the water where the sand is wet, cooler, and not as soft.

Ridged

● ● ● ● ● ● ● ● ● ● ● ● ● ● ● ● ● ●

Fingerprints are ridges on your fingertips that make up a special pattern

Purpose: To identify your fingerprint type.

Round Up These Things

pencil
1 index card
transparent tape
1 magnifying lens

Things to Do

1. Rub the lead of a pencil back and forth on the index card.

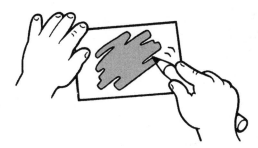

2. Rub the tip of one finger across the pencil marking.

3. Cover the smudged fingertip with a piece of transparent tape. Press the tape firmly against your finger.

4. Carefully remove the tape and press the sticky side to the box labeled "Fingerprint" on the Ridged answer sheet.

5. Use the magnifying lens to study the print.

6. Use the diagram of basic fingerprints to identify your type.

7. Compare your print pattern with others in your class.

BASIC FINGERPRINT PATTERNS

whorl

loop

arch

Ridged

● ● ● ● ● ● ● ● ● ● ● ● ● ● ● ● ● ● ●

Data:

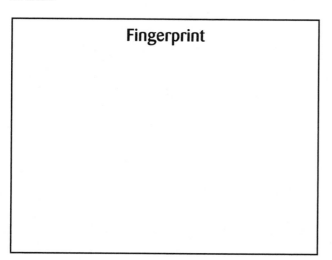

Fingerprint

Directions: Circle the letter in front of the statement that identifies your fingerprint type.

Results:

1. **A.** My fingerprint design is an arch.

   B. My fingerprint design is a loop.

   C. My fingerprint design is a whorl.

Directions: Circle the letter in front of the statement of the best conclusion.

Conclusion:

2. **A.** Everyone has the same fingerprint design.

   B. Each person has a different fingerprint design.

   C. Even though no one else has exactly the same fingerprint as me, there are basic types of fingerprints.

Communication

Communication means to pass along information. You communicate in many ways, such as when you talk, act something out, write, draw pictures, make a model, or make a chart. Information that is recorded is called data.

Model

Benchmarks

By the end of grade 2, students should be able to
- Identify different ways of communicating.
- Develop an understanding of the life cycles of organisms.
- Develop an understanding of how insects grow.

In this chapter, students are expected to
- Demonstrate communication by modeling— acting out.
- Demonstrate knowledge of metamorphoses of a butterfly by acting out the change.
- Demonstrate how grasshoppers grow by modeling the molting process.

Preparing the Materials

Activity 1: Pass It On
- Make a copy of the Pass It On activity sheets for each student.
- Make crayons and/or markers available for each student.
- Prepare an area where groups of students can act out a four-legged animal.

Activity 2: Fly Away
- Make a copy of the Fly Away activity instruction sheet for each student or group.
- Make a sleeping bag and two colored scarves available for the class or each group. You may wish for one student to demonstrate the acting out of the changes that occur. Then, one group of students at a time can use the materials with each person in the group taking turns being the actor.

Activity 3: Dancing Bees
- Make a copy of the Dancing Bees activity instruction sheets for each student or group.
- Prepare 28 shoe prints—14 colored left shoe prints and 14 white right shoe prints. Make an

outline of one of your students' shoes on a piece of stiff paper, such as poster board. Cut out the shoe outline. Stack seven sheets of white copy paper. Lay the shoe pattern on the top sheet. Trace the pattern twice, then cut out the two outlines, cutting through all seven layers. Repeat using colored copy paper.
- Use a marker to number eight of the white shoe prints with odd numbers from 1 through 15. Number the remaining white shoe prints with odd numbers from 5 through 15.
- Number eight of the colored shoe prints with even numbers from 2 through 16. Number the remaining colored shoe prints with even numbers from 6 through 16.
- Lay the shoe prints on the floor in the pattern shown in the diagram on the investigation sheet. Use tape to secure the prints to the floor. This is the pattern of a bee's dance when food is far away.
- Stand an artificial flower, with any color petals except red, in a small flower pot of sand. Any safe unbreakable holder for the flower will work. Set the pot with the flower on the floor about 4 feet (1.2 m) from the dance pattern and in line with steps 1 through 4.

Investigation 1: Break Out
- Make a copy of the Break Out investigation instruction sheet for each group.
- Make a copy of the Break Out investigation answer sheet for each student.
- Have newspaper and cookies available for each group.
- Demonstrate the procedure, then allow the children to help one another. For very young children, you may wish to have them work in pairs as you read each step aloud to them.
- In this investigation, acting is used not only to discover science facts but to communicate the information to observers.
- Before the investigation, tell the class that the hard exoskeleton of insects cannot grow

larger. This means that the insect must get out of the small exoskeleton and make a new, bigger one.

Presenting the Science Concepts

1. Introduce the new terms:

   communication   To pass on information.

   model   (1) Something that is made to represent an object or a thing. (2) To communicate information by acting it out.

2. Explore the new terms:
   - The stages in the life cycle of a butterfly are egg, caterpillar, chrysalis, and adult.
   - The difference between a cocoon and a chrysalis is how the protective sac is made. A caterpillar makes its cocoon out of strands of its own silk. A chrysalis is a liquid coating made by the caterpillar that dries around the caterpillar's body. Generally, moths make cocoons and butterflies make chrysalises.
   - Young insects such as grasshoppers eat and grow larger, but their outer covering, called an **exoskeleton**, does not grow. When a grasshopper's exoskeleton gets too tight, it splits and the grasshopper wiggles out of it. The insect has a liquid covering its body that forms a new exoskeleton when dry.
   - One way to model an idea is by acting it out. Another way is to make something, such as a diagram or a three-dimensional (3-D) object.
   - A model can be a diagram or a picture of an existing object or system, such as the solar system.
   - A Venn diagram can be used to record information. Explain that the overlapping area of the circles contains information that is true about all the things the diagram represents.

- A model can be a 3-D structure, such as Styrofoam balls used to represent the position of the Sun and planets in our solar system.

EXTENSION

Students can make and compare models of the life cycles of a butterfly and a grasshopper.

Answers

Activity 1: Pass It On

1. Student drawing of a two-legged animal.
2. Student drawing of a four-legged animal.
3. Student answers will vary. Differences could be patterned fur and body size. Similarities could be the number of eyes and ears.
4. Student answers will vary, such as holding arms to their sides and waddling like a penguin; walking on their hands and knees and making sounds like a horse or another four-legged animal; and so on.

Activity 2: Fly Away

There are no incorrect answers. Students simply need to follow the directions.

Activity 3: Dancing Bees

There are no incorrect answers. Students simply need to follow the directions.

Investigation 1: Break Out

1. outer
2. exoskeleton
3. break
4. split open, wiggle out
5. splits open, wiggles out

© 2007 by John Wiley & Sons, Inc.

ACTIVITY 18

Pass It On

You collect information every day by making observations of the things around you. **Communication** means to pass along this information to others. One way to communicate is to **model**. Two types of models are a diagram, such as a drawing, and acting out the information.

Directions: Follow the instructions to make a model.

1. Draw and color a picture of an animal with two legs.

2. Draw and color a picture of an animal with four legs.

ACTIVITY 1

8

Pass It On (continued)

3. In the diagram, write or draw the ways the two animals are different and ways they are alike.

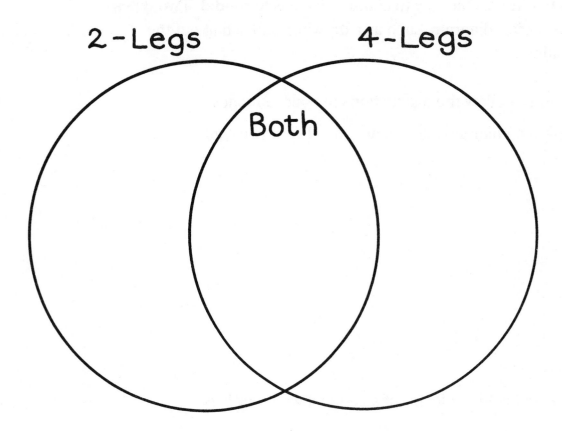

2-Legs   4-Legs

Both

4. Act out one of your animals.

Fly Away

● ●

Directions: Read about how caterpillars change into butterflies. Then follow the steps to act it out.

Some insects, such as butterflies, do not grow from smaller versions of themselves. Instead, a butterfly is full-grown when it breaks out of a special sac called a **chrysalis**. The chrysalis forms around the body of a **caterpillar**, which is a wormlike critter. Inside the chrysalis, the caterpillar forms itself into a butterfly. The butterfly breaks out of the chrysalis and flies away. Here's a way to act out this change.

1. Lay an open sleeping bag on the floor.

2. Place the scarves inside the top end of the bag.

3. Pretend to be a caterpillar and crawl inside the bag. Zip the bag closed over your body. The bag is your chrysalis.

4. Inside the chrysalis, find the scarves, and hold one in each hand. The scarves will be your wings.

5. Lie very still for a few seconds, then wiggle around as you unzip the bag.

6. Crawl out, stand, and walk around very slowly with your arms and the scarves hanging by your body. At first the butterfly is wet and has to dry.

7. Start slowly flapping your arms and the scarves. Then flap more quickly as you pretend to be a flying butterfly.

Dancing Bees

● ● ● ● ● ● ● ● ● ● ● ● ● ● ● ● ● ● ●

Directions: Read about how bees find nectar. Then follow the steps to act it out.

Bees eat nectar from flowers, and all of the bees that collect nectar are female. Bees tell one another where faraway food is by doing a waggle dance. First, the bee flies in a straight line that points toward the food. She flies in a circle around one side of the line to get back to her starting place, then retraces the straight line and flies in a circle around the other side. She moves from one side to the other, making a pattern that looks like the number 8. To show distance, she waggles her head and body, moving them quickly from side to side. The faster she waggles, the farther away the food is.

1. Facing the direction of the flower, stand with your right foot on the white number 1 shoe print and your left foot on the colored number 2 print.

2. Walk forward by placing your feet on prints 3 and 4. As you walk toward the flower, waggle by moving your head and body from side to side.

3. Step on print 5 on the left side of the pattern. Stop waggling and continue around the left side.

4. When you reach the centerline, start waggling and walk through the center again.

5. Step on print 5 on the right side of the pattern. Stop waggling and continue around the right side.

6. Follow the path several times and waggle only when you move through the center. You are doing a bee dance called the waggle dance.

Dancing Bees (continued)

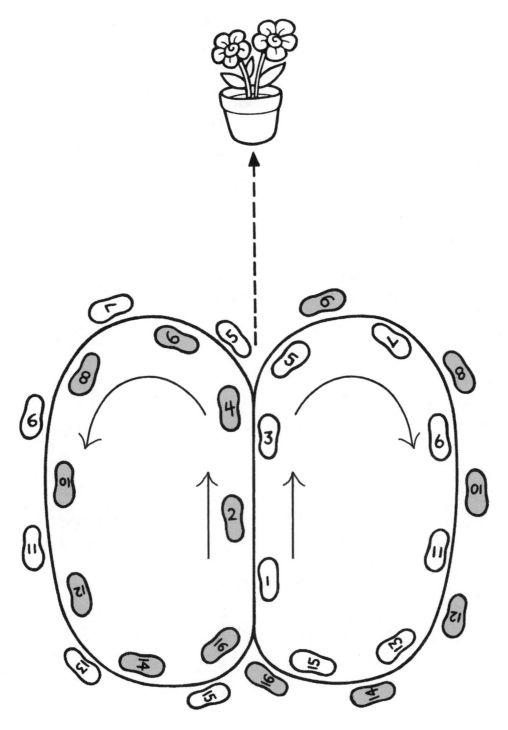

Break Out

• • • • • • • • • • • • • • • • • •

Purpose: To determine how insects break out of their **exoskeletons** (outer covering).

Round Up These Things

6 sheets of newspaper
transparent tape
1 cookie

Things to Do

1. Stand with your arms folded over your chest and pretend to be an insect.

2. Ask your helper to wrap two layers of newspaper around your body, one around your chest and the other around your hips. Ask your partner to use tape to secure the papers together. The paper is your exoskeleton.

3. Ask your partner to hold the cookie to your mouth so you can take a bite of it.

4. Eat the bite of cookie, then pretend to grow by pushing on the paper with your arms. The paper around your chest will tear apart, but the paper around your hips will stay together.

5. Wiggle your body so that the paper falls, then step out of the paper and leave it on the floor.

6. Follow directions on the Break Out answer sheet.

INVESTIGATION 1

8

Answer Sheet

Break Out

● ● ● ● ● ● ● ● ● ● ● ● ● ● ● ● ● ● ● ●

Directions: Circle the words that correctly complete each sentence.

Data:

1. An insect's exoskeleton is its _____ covering.

   inner   outer

2. When you pretended to be an insect, the paper wrapped around you was your _____ .

   exoskeleton   skin

3. As an insect, you had to grow to make your exoskeleton _____ .

   grow   break

Results:

4. When you pushed on the newspaper, it _____ and you were able to _____ .

   split open   puffed up   wiggle out   turn around

Conclusion:

5. When an insect's exoskeleton gets too small, the exoskeleton _____ and the insect _____.

   splits open   puffs up   wiggles out   turns around

Data

Benchmarks

By the end of grade 2, students should be able to

- Use patterns and sorting techniques to explore data.
- Use patterns to describe relationships and make predictions.
- Describe the order in which events occur.
- List things in order using ordinal numbers.

In this chapter, students are expected to

- Identify, describe, and extend patterns to make predictions and solve problems.
- Organize and interpret data.
- Construct picture graphs and bar graphs.
- Draw conclusions and answer questions based on picture graphs and bar graphs.

Preparing the Materials

Activity 1: Missing Word

- Make a copy of the Missing Word activity instruction and answer sheets for each student.

Activity 2: Ordinal Numbers

- Make a copy of the Ordinal Numbers activity sheet for each student.

Activity 3: Line Up

- Make a copy of the Line Up activity sheets for each student.
- Make crayons or markers available for each student.

Activity 4: Predictions

- Make a copy of the Predictions activity instruction and answer sheets for each student.
- Following the steps of the diagram, use poster board (65-pound or heavier paper) to make two connecting paper dolls for each student.
- Make crayons or markers available for each student.

Presenting the Science Concepts

1. Introduce the new terms:

   graph   A chart that compares two sets of data.

   interpret   Using data to explain something or to answer a question.

   ordinal number   A number used to tell the order in a series or a group.

   predict   To guess what you think will happen next.

2. Explore the new terms:

   - Compare the order and names of counting numbers and ordinal numbers: one (first), two (second), three (third), four (fourth), five (fifth), and so on.
   - Compare the symbol and name of the first ten ordinal numbers: first (1st), second (2nd), third (3rd), fourth (4th), fifth (5th), and so on.
   - A graph has one set of data on the vertical scale and the second set on the horizontal scale.

EXTENSION

Students can experiment with folding paper. They should fold the paper three times to check their prediction. They can also cut different patterns.

Answers

Activity 1: Missing Word

Part I: Collect the Data

1. fish
2. shoes
3. bananas

Part II: Interpret the Data

1. bananas
2. fish
3. Hayden

Activity 2: Ordinal Numbers

Part I: Place Winners

1. Rich—first place, the line should be drawn to the bird.
2. Hal—second place, the line should be drawn to the fish.
3. Gina—third place, the line should be drawn to the butterfly.

Part II: Stands For

1. 4th
2. 10th
3. 5th
4. 8th
5. 2nd
6. 9th
7. 6th

Activity 3: Line Up

Part I: Collecting Data

1. studying
2. insects

3. six
4. two
5. eight

Part II: Making a Graph

Stella—six colored boxes

Trae—two colored boxes

Tate—eight colored boxes

Part III: Using a Graph

1. Tate
2. Trae

Activity 4: Predictions

1. one
2. two

Prediction Data:

1. one
2. two
3. student prediction (four dolls are formed)

Missing Word

Data is information that you record. You collect data when you record what you observe. You **interpret** data when you use it to explain something or to answer a question.

Directions: In the table, check the box under the missing word that completes the sentence. Then use the table to answer the questions. Circle the correct answer. This example is done for you.

Example:

First Part of the Sentence	Missing Word				
	Spiders	Fish	Knees	Bananas	Shoes
Chris is reading a book about	✔				

1. What does Chris like to read about?

(spiders)   fish   bananas   shoes

© 2007 by John Wiley & Sons, Inc.

ACTIVITY 1
9
Answer Sheet

Missing Word

● ● ● ● ● ● ● ● ● ● ● ● ● ● ● ● ● ● ● ●

Part I: Collect the Data

Directions: Look at the pictures in the table. Read the sentence parts. Then check the box under the missing word that completes each sentence.

First Part of the Sentence	Missing Word				
	Spider	Fish	Knees	Bananas	Shoes
1. Mary's pet is a					
2. Hayden has a new pair of					
3. Raygan likes to eat					

ACTIVITY 1

9

Answer Sheet

Missing Word (continued)

● ●

Part II: Interpret the Data

I. Directions: Use the table on the Missing Word answer sheet (Part I) to answer the following questions. Circle the correct answer.

1. What kind of fruit does Raygan like to eat?

apples   oranges   bananas

2. What kind of pet does Mary have?

cat   fish   dog

3. Who has new shoes?

Mary   Hayden   Chris

II. Directions: Use the table on the Missing Word answer sheet (Part I) to draw a picture of Mary's pet.

Ordinal Numbers

Ordinal numbers are used to tell the order in a series, such as first or second.

Part I: Place Winners

Directions: Look at the pictures. Then identify who drew each picture by drawing a line from the picture to the name of the child who drew it.

1. Rich—first place

2. Hal—second place

3. Gina—third place

Part II: Stands For

Directions: Write the symbol for each ordinal number in the blank. The first one is done for you.

1. fourth ___4th___

2. tenth _____

3. fifth _____

4. eighth _____

5. second _____

6. ninth _____

7. sixth _____

ACTIVITY 3

9 Line Up

A **graph** is a chart that compares two sets of data. Graphs can be made by using drawings.

Part I: Collecting Data

Directions: Stella, Trae, and Tate are observers. Study their pictures. Then circle the word that completes each sentence.

1. An observer is a person who is _____ something.

   studying   writing   painting

2. Stella, Trae, and Tate are studying _____ .

   birds   snakes   insects

3. Stella is studying _____ butterflies.

   two   four   six   eight

4. Trae is observing _____ beetles.

   two   four   six   eight

5. Tate is observing _____ crickets.

   two   four   six   eight

Stella

Tate

Trae

ACTIVITY 3

Line Up (continued)

Part II: Making a Graph

Directions: Color the number of boxes to show how many insects each person is studying.

Observers

Number of Bugs

| Stella | Trae | Tate |

Part III: Using a Graph

Directions: Use your graph to find the answer to the following questions.

1. Who is observing the most bugs? _____

2. Who is observing the fewest bugs? _____

Predictions

To **predict** is to guess what you think will happen next.

Directions: Read about making paper dolls. Look at the pictures. Then follow the instructions on the answer sheet.

Paper Dolls

1. A sheet of paper is folded in half and a pattern of half of a doll is drawn on one side as shown. The pattern is cut out and unfolded.

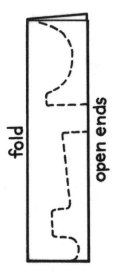

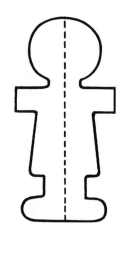

2. A sheet of paper is folded in half two times. The same doll pattern as before is drawn, cut out, and unfolded.

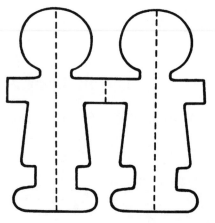

Predictions

● ● ● ● ● ● ● ● ● ● ● ● ● ● ● ● ● ● ● ●

Results:

Directions: Circle the correct answers to the questions.

Paper dolls are cut from paper folded once.

1. How many paper dolls are formed?

   one   two   three   four

Paper dolls are cut from paper folded two times.

2. How many paper dolls are formed?

   one   two   three   four

Make a Prediction

Directions: Predict how many paper dolls will be formed if the instructions below are followed. Circle your prediction.

A sheet of paper is folded in half three times. The same doll pattern as before is drawn, cut out, and unfolded.

3. Predict how many paper dolls will be formed.

   one   two   three   four

Making and Using Definitions

A *definition* is a statement that explains the meaning of a word, a phrase, or a symbol. A *dictionary* is a book that contains an alphabetical list of words with their definitions. A *glossary* is a short alphabetical list of definitions in the back of a book. An understanding of how to find definitions, as well as make them, gives kids the tools they will need to accurately record scientific observations.

New Words

Benchmarks

By the end of grade 2, students should be able to
- Learn new vocabulary words through reading.
- Use knowledge of word order (syntax) and context to confirm word meaning.
- Discuss meanings of words and develop vocabulary through meaningful/concrete experiences.
- Use context to identify the meaning of words.

In this chapter, students are expected to
- Complete definitions.
- Use definitions to draw an image of bean parts.
- Observe and identify bean parts.
- Answer riddles.

Preparing the Materials

Activity 1: Definitions
- Make a copy of the Definitions activity sheets for each student.

Activity 2: Learning New Words
- Make a copy of the Learning New Words activity sheet for each student.
- Make crayons or markers available for each student.

Activity 3: Words Only
- Make a copy of the Words Only activity sheet for each student.

Investigation 1: Bean Parts
- Make a copy of the Bean Parts investigation instruction and answer sheets for each student.
- Soak six pinto beans per group in water overnight. Keep the beans refrigerated so that they do not spoil before the students use them. Drain the beans before use.
- Make available each student's completed Words Only activity sheet.

Activity 4: Inference—Riddles
- Make a copy of the Inference—Riddles activity sheet for each student.

Presenting the Science Concepts

1. Introduce the new terms:

   definition A statement explaining the meaning of a word.

   inference A guess about something based on what you already know.

   riddle A puzzle made of words that form a question that needs an answer.

2. Explore the new terms:
   - Some definitions are not complete without a picture. For example, both a tiger and a zebra can be defined as animals with stripes.
   - Compare predicting and inferring. Predicting is guessing what will happen next. Inferring is guessing about what has happened or is happening now. For example, if you see lightning, you can predict that in a short time you will hear thunder. If you hear thunder, you can infer that there was a bolt of lightning, even if you did not see it.

EXTENSION

Students can use definitions to write riddles. For example:

- Definition
  ice cream A cold, sweet food.
- Riddle
  I am cold. I am sweet.
  I taste good.
  What am I?

ANSWERS

Activity 1: Definitions

1. air
2. water
3. animal
4. crush
5. taste
6. light
7. hit

Activity 2: Learning New Words

Student drawing of a cat (or other animal) with whiskers.

Activity 3: Words Only

Student drawings of the parts of a seed from the definition only. (This is not expected to be accurate.)

Investigation 1: Bean Parts

Student answers may very. Expected answers are:

1. A
2. A
3. A
4. B

Activity 4: Inference—Riddles

1. teeth
2. dragon
3. snake
4. butterfly

ACTIVITY 1

10 **Definitions**

A **definition** is a statement explaining the meaning of a word.

Directions: Choose the word that completes each definition. Circle the word.

1. A soap bubble is filled with _____.

water   air   soap

2. A boat is used to travel on _____.

water   air   soap

3. Insects are a type of _____.

plant   animal   rock

4. Teeth are used to _____ food.

crush   grow   find

ACTIVITY 1

10 **Definitions** (continued)

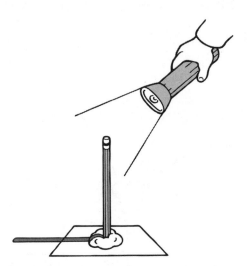

5. Sour is a kind of _____.

    smell   touch   taste

6. A shadow forms when an object blocks _____.

    light   air   people

7. Wind chimes make music when the hanging parts _____ one another.

    stick   hit   sing

ACTIVITY 2

10 Learning New Words

In books, some words are printed in dark letters. These are new words you need to learn. When you read the sentence the dark printed word is in, you will learn what the word means.

To help you remember what a word means, write down its definition. Then draw a picture of the word. In the following example, *flower* is the new word.

Example:

Plant Parts

Plants are made of different parts. A **flower** is the part of a plant where seeds are made.

Directions: Read the story. Then, in the box, complete the definition. Draw a picture for the definition of the new word.

Cat Whiskers

Whiskers are hairs that grow on an animal's face. Cats have about 24 long whiskers. There are about 12 whiskers on each side of a cat's face.

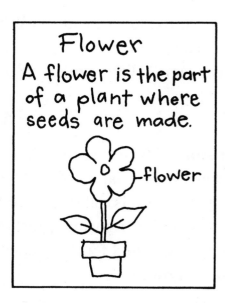

Flower
A flower is the part of a plant where seeds are made.

-flower

Whiskers

Whiskers are _____

that grow on an

animal's _____ .

ACTIVITY 3
10
Words Only

Directions: Read about a bean. Guess what you think the different bean parts look like. Then, in the box below, draw the different bean parts. Draw a line from each drawing to the word that matches it.

A Bean

A **bean** is a type of seed. The covering on the outside of a bean is called a **seed coat**. Inside each bean is a structure that looks like a baby plant and is called the **seed plant**. The seed plant grows into a new plant. The remaining part of the inside of the bean is stored food, called **seed food**. When planted, the seed plant uses the seed food to grow.

Seed coat	Seed plant	Seed food

© 2007 by John Wiley & Sons, Inc.

Bean Parts

Purpose: To determine what the seed coat, seed plant, and seed food of a bean look like.

Round Up These Things

6 presoaked beans
1 paper towel
your Words Only activity sheet
1 flashlight
1 magnifying lens

Things to Do

1. Place the 6 beans on the paper towel.

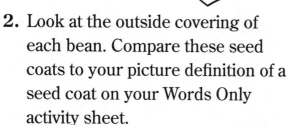

2. Look at the outside covering of each bean. Compare these seed coats to your picture definition of a seed coat on your Words Only activity sheet.

3. With your fingernail, scratch off the seed coat of one of the beans.

4. Holding the bean in your

hands, pry apart the two parts of the bean with your fingers.

5. Repeat steps 2 through 4 with the other beans.

6. Hold the lit flashlight on each bean as you observe its inside with the magnifying lens.

7. Look for the seed plant in each bean. The seed plant is a tiny, colorless, plantlike structure. Compare the seed plant to your picture definition of a seed plant.

8. Look for the seed food in each bean. The seed food is the remaining part of the bean. Compare the seed food to your picture definition of seed food.

Bean Parts

Directions: Circle the correct letter in front of the correct ending to each sentence.

Results:

1. My seed coat drawing is

   A. different from what a seed coat looks like.

   B. similar to what a seed coat looks like.

2. My seed plant drawing is

   A. different from what a seed plant looks like.

   B. similar to what a seed plant looks like.

3. My seed food drawing is

   A. different from what seed food looks like.

   B. similar to what seed food looks like.

Directions: Circle the letter in front of the sentence that best describes your conclusion for this investigation.

Conclusion:

4. In order to draw a correct picture of an object,

   A. you have to have a word description so you know what it looks like.

   B. you have to observe it so you know what it looks like.

ACTIVITY 4

Inference—Riddles

An **inference** is a guess about something based on what you already know. A **riddle** is a puzzle made of words that form a question that needs an answer. The words give you clues so you can infer the answer to the riddle.

Directions: Choose a word from the list below to answer each riddle.

butterfly   teeth   dragon   snake

1. I am little. I am hard.

You need me to eat.

What am I?

_____

- -

_____

2. I can fly and breathe fire.

But I am not real.

What am I?

_____

- -

_____

3. People scream when they see me.

I can slither.

What am I?

_____

- -

_____

4. I used to be a worm. Now I can fly.

I am very colorful.

What am I?

_____

- -

_____

Benchmarks

By the end of grade 2, students should be able to
- Demonstrate knowledge of alphabetical order.
- Develop vocabulary through reading.
- Use resources and references, such as beginners' dictionaries, to understand word meanings.
- Use glossaries to understand word meanings.

In this chapter, students are expected to
- Use pages from a picture dictionary to answer questions.
- List words in ABC order.
- Use the text and a glossary to answer questions.

Preparing the Materials

Activity 1: ABC Order
- Make a copy of the ABC Order activity sheet for each student.

Activity 2: Using a Dictionary
- Make a copy of the Using a Dictionary activity instruction and answer sheets for each student.

Activity 3: Make a Picture Dictionary
- Make a copy of the Make a Picture Dictionary instruction and activity sheets for each student.
- Make scissors, glue or tape, string, and crayons or markers available for each student.
- Make thirteen unlined index cards available for each student.
- With a paper hole punch, cut a hole in the center near the edge of one short side of each card.

Activity 4: Using a Glossary
- Make a copy of the Using a Glossary activity sheets for each student.

- Make a copy of the Big-Hearted booklet sheet for each student.
- Prepare a Big-Hearted booklet for each student. Do this by cutting around the outside lines of the booklet. Then fold the booklet in half twice so that the pages are in order. The title page will be the front of the booklet. The booklet will open to pages 1 and 2, with page 3 on the back.
- Make crayons or markers available for each student.

Presenting the Science Concepts

1. Introduce the new terms:

   ABC order   A word list in order of the alphabet.

   dictionary   A book that contains words in ABC order with their definitions.

   glossary   A short list of definitions in ABC order at the back of a book.

   picture dictionary   A dictionary with definitions and pictures to explain the meaning of words.

2. Explore the new terms:
   - ABC order, or alphabetical order, is the order that the letters of the alphabet are arranged.
   - It is easier to find things if they are in ABC order. For example, it would be difficult to find words in a dictionary if the words were in no particular order.
   - The words in a glossary are usually the new words introduced in a book.

EXTENSION

A real heart is not shaped like a Valentine's Day heart. Instead, it is shaped more like an upside-down pear. Have students hold an artificial pear upside down and look at its shape. Then make a drawing of a person with an upside-down pear-shaped heart. Remind the students that the heart is in the center of the chest with the pointed bottom tilted a little toward the left side of the chest. Point out that the left and right on a picture are reversed.

ANSWERS

Activity 1: ABC Order

1. bug
2. clock
3. flower

Activity 2: Using a Dictionary

1. baby
2. bandage
3. bark

4. bird
5. bones

Activity 3: Make a Picture Dictionary

The pictures and words in the dictionary should be in this order: alligator, bulldog, chameleon, fish, flea, frog, horse, monkey, octopus, parrot, rabbit, spider.

Activity 4: Using a Glossary

1. fist
2. top
3. bottom
4. blood
5. hand
6. blood
7. belly
8. oxygen

ACTIVITY 11

ABC Order

Words listed in the order of the alphabet are in **ABC order**. This means that a word starting with the letter *A* comes first. Words starting with the letter *B* come next, and so on, in the order of the alphabet.

Directions: Circle the first letter of each word in the list. Then write the words in ABC order in the spaces on the left side of the paper. To the right of each word, draw a picture of what that word describes.

clock   flower   bug

1. _____

_____

2. _____

_____

3. _____

_____

ACTIVITY 2

11

Instruction Sheet

Using a Dictionary

● ● ● ● ● ● ● ● ● ● ● ● ● ● ● ● ● ● ●

A **dictionary** is a book that gives the meaning of words. Words in a dictionary are in ABC order. A **picture dictionary** has a picture for each word that is defined.

Directions: Look at the picture definitions. Then, on the Using a Dictionary answer sheet, write the word that answers each sentence.

baby
A very young child.

bandage
A covering for a wound.

bark
The sound a dog makes.

bee
An insect that stings.

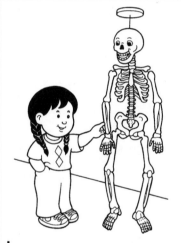

bird
An animal that has feathers.

bite
To cut into food with your teeth.

bones
The hard body parts that hold the body upright.

boy
A young male person.

Using a Dictionary

1. What do you call a very young child?

_____

- -

_____

2. What is a covering for a wound called?

_____

- -

_____

3. What sound does a dog make?

_____

- -

_____

4. What is an animal with feathers?

_____

- -

_____

5. What parts of your body are hard and hold you upright?

_____

- -

_____

Make a Picture Dictionary

ABC order, or *alphabetical order,* means to be arranged in order of the alphabet. The first letter of a word is used to put words in ABC order. Words in the dictionary are in ABC order.

Directions:

1. Write your name and My Picture Dictionary on an index card as shown. This is the title card.

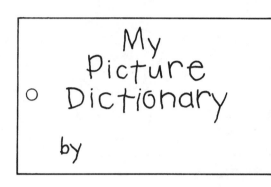

2. Cut out all the picture strips on pages 128 and 129. Glue one picture strip on the front of each index card as shown. Color the pictures.

Front

3. Cut out all the definition strips on pages 130 and 131. Glue each definition strip to the back of the picture card it explains.

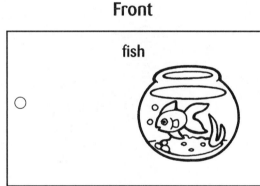

Back

4. Stack the cards in ABC order, front side up. Place the title card on top. Tie the cards together with a string.

Make a Picture Dictionary
(continued)

rabbit

bulldog

chameleon

flea

frog

horse

Make a Picture Dictionary

(continued)

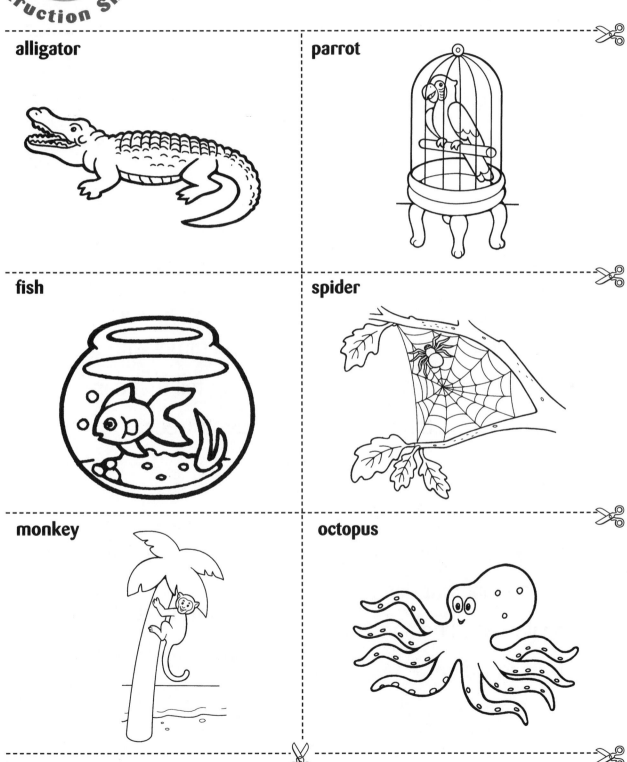

alligator

parrot

fish

spider

monkey

octopus

Make a Picture Dictionary

(continued)

● ● ● ● ● ● ● ● ● ● ● ● ● ● ● ● ● ● ●

An animal that lives in water and has many arms.

An animal with eight legs that spins a web.

An insect that bites other animals and makes them itch.

An animal with a very long tail that can climb trees.

An animal that has scales and fins and lives in water.

An animal that can hop long distances.

Make a Picture Dictionary
(continued)

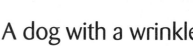

An animal that can be ridden.

A dog with a wrinkled face.

A small animal with very long ears.

An animal that can fly and learn to talk.

An animal that can change colors.

An animal with a long scaly body and tail, and a huge mouth with big teeth.

ACTIVITY 4

11

Using a Glossary

A **glossary** is a list of definitions in ABC order at the end of a book.

Directions: Read the Big-Hearted booklet your teacher gives you and do the Heart Experiment on page 1. Use the booklet to complete each statement below. If you have time when you're done, you can color the booklet.

1. Your heart is about as big as your _____

_____

_____

2. Your heart is wider at the _____

_____

_____

3. Your heart is more pointed at the _____

_____

_____

4. Your heart pumps _____

_____

_____

© 2007 by John Wiley & Sons, Inc.

Using a Glossary (continued)

Directions: Use the Big-Hearted Booklet's glossary to complete the definition of the terms.

5. fist

A tightly closed

_____

_____

6. heart

The part of the body that pumps

_____

_____

7. chest

The part of the body between the neck and the

_____

_____

8. blood

The liquid that carries

_____

_____

ACTIVITY 4

11

Using a Glossary (continued)

2

Your **heart** pumps blood. **Blood** carries nutrients and oxygen to all parts of the body. Your heart is about as big as your fist. Your heart is wider at the top and more pointed at the bottom. It lies in the center of your **chest** (the part of your body between your neck and belly) with its bottom tilted a little toward the left side of your chest.

1

Heart Experiment

1. Close your left hand to make a **fist**.

2. Hold your fist in the center of your chest.

3

Glossary

blood   The liquid that carries oxygen to all parts of the body.

chest   The part of your body between your neck and belly.

fist   A hand that is tightly closed.

heart   The part of the body that pumps blood.

Big-Hearted

Measuring and Estimating

Measure and *measurement* are words that describe the process of finding the amount of something, including its length, size, weight, and temperature. Both standard and nonstandard units can be used as measurements. *Standard units* are those measurements that are commonly accepted, such as inch, cup, liter, gram, pound, degrees Fahrenheit, and degrees Celsius. Instruments, such as a ruler, a measuring cup, a scale, or a thermometer are used to measure amounts in standard units.

Nonstandard units can be randomly decided on. For example, the width of a book can be measured in paper clips. Anything, including parts of your body, such as your hands, fingers, and feet, can be used as a nonstandard unit of measurement.

Estimating a measurement means to guess the amount of something without using a measuring instrument. The best way to develop the mathematical skill of measuring is by hands-on experience.

Length

Benchmarks

By the end of grade 2, students should be able to
- Measure length in nonstandard and standard units.
- Recognize and use models that approximate standard units (metric and English) of length.
- Use standard tools to measure length.
- Estimate measurements of length.

In this chapter, students are expected to
- Identify standard and nonstandard units of measurement.

Preparing the Materials

Activity 1: Length Units
- Make a copy of the Length Units activity instruction and answer sheets for each student.
- Make yellow, red, and green crayons available for each student.

Activity 2: Distance Measurements
- Make a copy of the Distance Measurements activity sheet for each student.

Activity 3: Royal Feet
- Make a copy of the Royal Feet activity sheet for each student.
- Make a 12-inch (30-cm) ruler available for each student.

Activity 4: Estimate
- Make a copy of the Estimate activity instruction and answer sheets for each student.

Investigation 1: How Big?
Make a copy of the How Big? instruction sheet for each student.

- Students should work in groups of two or more.
- Make a yardstick and a meter stick available for each group.

Presenting the Science Concepts

1. Introduce the new terms:

   centimeter (cm)   A metric unit of distance that is shorter than a meter. There are 100 centimeters in 1 meter.

   estimate   A guess about the amount of something without measuring it.

   foot (ft)   An English unit of distance that is shorter than a yard. There are 3 feet in 1 yard.

   height   The measure of the distance from the top to bottom of something that is standing upright.

   inch (in)   An English unit of distance that is shorter than a foot. There are 12 inches in 1 foot.

   kilometer (km)   A metric unit of distance longer than a meter. There are 1,000 meters in a kilometer.

   length   The measure of the distance between two points. The measure of the longest side of an object; equal to or longer than the width.

   measure   To find the amount of something.

   meter (m)   A metric unit of distance that is longer than a centimeter. There are 100 centimeters in a meter.

   nonstandard unit of measurement   Unit of measurement that is not commonly used.

   ruler   An instrument used to measure distance.

   standard unit of measurement   Unit found on a measuring tool.

   width   The measure of distance from one side to the other of something. The measure of the distance from side to side of an object; equal to or shorter than the length.

   yard (yd)   An English unit of distance that is longer than a foot. There are 3 feet in 1 yard.

TEACHING TIPS (continued)

2. Explore the new terms:

- Standard units of length in the English measurement system include the inch (in), the foot (ft), and the yard (yd).
- Standard units of length in the metric measurement system include the centimeter (cm), the meter (m), and the kilometer (km).
- Standard measuring tools include a ruler, a yardstick, a meter stick, a tape measure, and a carpenter's rule.
- One inch is about 2½ times as long as 1 cm.
- One yard is three times as long as 1 foot.
- Nonstandard units are those not commonly used. Any object can be used as a measuring tool. But you must repeatedly use the same object or many of the same objects placed end-to-end. For example, paper clips placed end-to-end or hooked together to form a chain can be used to measure the width of a book. The width might be 10 paper clips.
- The two measurements of a sheet of paper lying on a table are its length and width. If the paper were held vertically, the two measurements would be called height and width.

EXTENSION

Form a bar graph using the students' paper strips from Investigation 1: How Big? Do this by displaying the strips in order of length. Add a title and label the vertical and horizontal axes. For the vertical label, use a picture of a different color hat for each length. Ask the students questions about the graph, such as:

How many students wear a red hat? A blue hat? And so on.

ANSWERS

Activity 1: Length Units

- The two flowers on the left should be colored with red petals and yellow centers.
- The two flowers on the right should be colored with yellow petals and red centers.
- The stems and leaves of all the flowers should be colored green.

Activity 2: Distance Measurements

1. 4 inches

2. 3 inches

3. 2 inches

4. 5 centimeters

5. 4 centimeters

6. 3 centimeters

Activity 3: Royal Feet

Student answers will vary.

Activity 4: Estimate

1. Student answers will vary.

2. Student answers will depend on length of room.

3–8. Student answers will vary.

Investigation 1: How Big?

1. Student answers will vary.

ACTIVITY 1

12

Instruction Sheet

Length Units

● ●

To **measure** means to find the amount of something. **Length** is the measure of distance between two points. **Standard units of measurement** are those found on measuring tools, such as a **ruler**, a yardstick, a meter stick, or a carpenter's rule. **Nonstandard units of measurement** are not found on measuring tools and may be any object, including paper clips or even parts of your body, such as your foot.

Standard units for length include English and metric units.

English Units

inch (in)

foot (ft)

yard (yd)

Metric Units

centimeter (cm)

meter (m)

kilometer (km)

ACTIVITY 1
12
Answer Sheet

Length Units

● ● ● ● ● ● ● ● ● ● ● ● ● ● ● ● ● ●

Directions: Color the different parts of the flowers as described below.

yellow—spaces with standard English units

red—spaces with standard metric units

green—spaces with nonstandard units

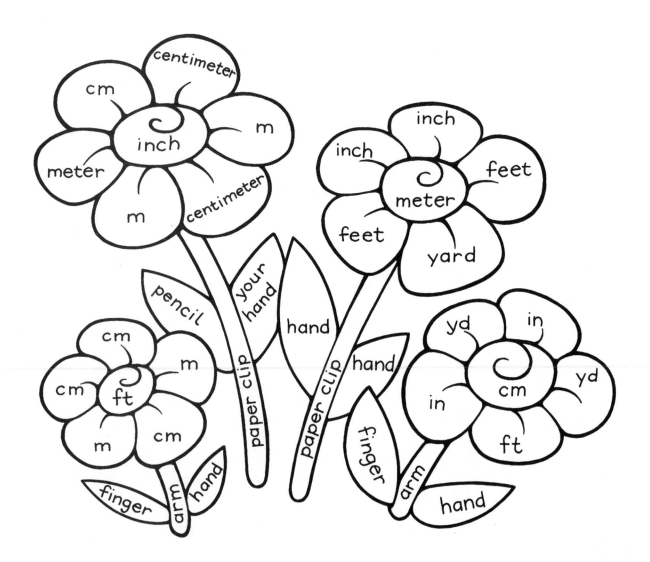

ACTIVITY 2

Distance Measurements

Height is the distance from the top to bottom of something. **Width** is the distance from one side to the other of something.

Directions: Use a ruler to measure the height of each picture frame in inches.

1. _____ inches   2. _____ inches   3. _____ inches

Directions: Use a ruler to measure the width of each picture frame in centimeters.

4. _____ centimeters   5. _____ centimeters   6. _____ centimeters

2

ACTIVITY 3

12   Royal Feet

On a ruler, 1 foot is equal to 12 inches (30 cm). This measurement is called a foot because, in the olden days, the length of the English king's foot was used to measure things. Your foot is probably not a foot long. Some people have feet that are as long as a ruler. Some people have feet that are longer than a ruler.

Directions: Follow the steps to discover the length of your foot.

1. Lay a 12-inch (30-cm) ruler on the floor.

2. Take off your right shoe.

3. Stand with your right heel at the beginning of the ruler. Does your foot reach all the way to the end of the ruler? _____

4. Ask a helper to measure the length of your foot to the nearest inch. The length of your foot is about _____ inches.

5. Ask a helper to measure the length of your foot to the nearest centimeter. The length of your foot is about _____ centimeters.

Estimate

An **estimate** is a guess about the amount of something without measuring it. The length of your foot will be called a royal foot in this activity.

Directions: Follow the instructions. Record your answers on the Room Length Data table on the Estimate answer sheet.

1. Estimate the length of a room in royal feet.

2. Use your feet to measure the room.

   • Remove your shoes.

   • Stand with the heel of one foot against the wall and place the heel of your other foot against your toes. This length is two royal feet from the wall.

   • Lift the back foot and place its heel against the toes of the other foot. This position is three royal feet from the wall.

   • Continue to move in a straight line across the room, counting each royal foot. Count the last royal foot only if it is at least half the length of your foot.

← 2 royal feet →

Estimate

● ●

Room Length Data	
Activity	Room Length (royal feet)
1. Estimate the length of the room.	
2. Measure the length of the room.	

Directions: Compare your estimated length with your measurement length of the room. Then write T in the blank if the statement is true. Write F in the blank if the statement is false.

3. The estimated length is longer than the measured length. _____

4. The estimated length is shorter than the measured length. _____

5. The estimated length is equal to the measured length. _____

Directions: Write the name of another student in the data table. Write the student's measured room length in the data table.

Room Length Data II	
Name	Room Length (royal feet)

Directions: Compare your measured length of the room in royal feet with the student's measurement. Then write T in the blank if the statement is true. Write F in the blank if the statement is false.

6. My measurement is larger. _____

7. My measurement is smaller. _____

8. The measurements are equal. _____

How Big?

Purpose: To determine how big around your head is.

Round Up These Things

1 narrow strip of paper
1 pencil
1 yardstick
1 meter stick

Things to Do

1. Ask a helper to prepare a measuring strip by following these steps:

   • Wrap the paper strip around your head across your forehead so that the ends of the paper overlap.

   • Holding the overlapping ends together, remove the paper strip from your head.

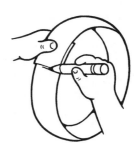

   • Use the pencil to make a mark where the ends of the paper overlap.

2. Measure the distance around your head by following these steps:

   • Lay the paper strip flat on a table. Write your name on the strip.

   • Use the yardstick to measure the length in inches of the paper from the end where you started to the mark. Record your measurement on the paper strip.

   • Use a meter stick to measure the length in centimeters of the paper from the end where you started to the mark. Record your measurement on the paper strip.

Capacity

Benchmarks

By the end of grade 2, students should be able to
- Recognize and use models that approximate standard units (metric and English) of capacity.
- Use standard tools to measure capacity.

In this chapter, students are expected to
- Use measuring tools to determine volume measurements.
- Predict volumes.
- Use "less than" and "greater than" symbols.

Preparing the Materials

Activity 1: Picture Problems—Same As
- Make a copy of the Picture Problems—Same As activity sheet for each student or group.

Investigation 1: Poppers
- Make a copy of the Poppers investigation sheet for each student or group.
- Prepare 1 plastic resealable bag containing 10 unpopped popcorn kernels for each group.
- Prepare 1 paper lunch sack for each group. Place 13 pieces of popped popcorn in the bags to reinforce subtraction. Draw a Do Not Eat symbol on each sack.
- Because popcorn is so tempting to eat, you may wish to have a popcorn snack after the investigation is completed.

Activity 2: How Much?
- Make a copy of the How Much? activity instruction and answer sheets for each student.
- Each student will need three large index cards or pieces of poster board.
- Make a red crayon available for each student.

Presenting the Science Concepts

1. Introduce the new terms:

   capacity   How much something will hold.

   cup (c)   A standard unit of measuring capacity that is smaller than a quart. There are 4 cups in 1 quart.

   gallon (gal)   A standard unit of measuring capacity that is larger than a quart. There are 4 quarts in a gallon.

   liter (L)   A standard metric unit of measuring capacity.

   milliliter (mL)   A standard metric unit of measuring capacity that is smaller than a liter. There are 1,000 milliliters in 1 liter.

   quart (qt)   A standard unit of measuring capacity that is smaller than a gallon.

   tablespoon (tbs)   A standard unit of measuring capacity that is larger than a teaspoon.

   teaspoon (tsp)   A standard unit of measuring capacity that is smaller than a tablespoon. There are 3 teaspoons in 1 tablespoon.

2. Explore the new terms:
   - Capacity is also called volume.
   - Size is often used to describe the capacity of objects, such as popped popcorn.
   - The standard capacity units in the English system include the cup, the gallon, the quart, the tablespoon, and the teaspoon.
   - The standard capacity units in the metric system include the liter and the milliliter.
   - One liter is about the same amount as one quart.

EXTENSION

1. After completing Activity 1, Picture Problems—Same As, students can compare the capacity of different measuring tools, such as measuring spoons and measuring cups. Students can also compare the capacity of different containers, such as quart, liter, and gallon jars.

2. Demonstrate the amount of blood in a baby, a child, and an adult as described in the How Much? activity. Do this by filling nine quart jars with water. Add about 10 drops of red food coloring to each jar. Stir. Make stand-up cards using the procedure in the How Much? activity, or borrow cards from students. Separate the jars into groups of one jar, three jars, and five jars. Place the appropriate stand-up card in front of each group of jars.

ANSWERS

Activity 1: Picture Problems—Same As

1. 1 gal
2. 1 qt
3. 4 qts
4. 1 qt
5. 1 tbs

Investigation 1: Poppers

3. 13
4. 3
6. Popped popcorn kernels take up more space.
7. increases

Activity 2: How Much?

1. 5
2. 3
3. 1
4. > (greater than)
5. < (less than)
6. < (less than)
7. > (geater than)
8. adult
9. baby

ACTIVITY 1

13

Picture Problems—Same As

Capacity is how much something will hold. The standard units of measuring capacity include **milliliter (mL)**, **teaspoon (tsp)**, **table-spoon (tbs)**, **cup (c)**, **quart (qt)**, **gallon (gal)**, and **liter (L)**.

This is how the measurements compare:

    1 teaspoon = 5 milliliters

    3 teaspoons = 1 tablespoon

    4 cups = 1 quart

    4 quarts = 1 gallon

    1 quart = about 1 liter

Directions: Use the symbols shown to represent the answer.

tsp   tbs   cup   qt   L   gal

Example: 5 mL = <u>1 tsp</u>

1. 4 qts = _____

2. 1 L = about _____

3. 1 gal = _____

4. 4 cups = _____

5. 3 tsp = _____

Poppers

Purpose: To show how heat affects the size of popcorn kernels.

Round Up These Things

1 paper towel
1 paper sack of popped popcorn
1 plastic bag with 10 unpopped
  popcorn kernels
two 5-ounce (150-mL) paper cups

Things to Do

1. Lay the paper towel on a table.

2. Pour the popped popcorn from the paper bag onto the paper towel.

3. Count the pieces of popcorn on the towel.

   • How many pieces of popcorn were in the paper sack? _____

4. You want to have only 10 pieces of popped popcorn on the towel.

   • How many pieces of popcorn do you need to subtract to have 10? _____

5. Count out 10 pieces of popped corn and put them in one of the paper cups.

6. Count out 10 unpopped popcorn kernels from the plastic bag and put them in the other paper cup. Which take up more space in the cup, popped or unpopped popcorn kernels?

   _____

Conclusion: Circle the word that correctly completes the sentence.

7. When popcorn kernels are heated, their size _____.

   increases   decreases

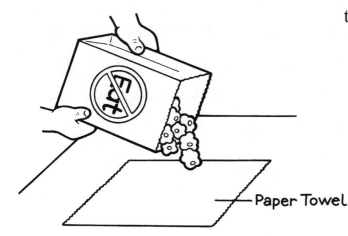

Paper Towel

How Much?

Blood is a liquid that carries oxygen and **nutrients** to all parts of the body. Nutrients are substances that living organisms need for life and growth. A baby has less blood than a child or an adult. As the baby grows, its body increases in size and the capacity of blood in its body increases, too.

Directions: Make a stand-up card to show about how many quarts (liters) of blood are in a baby, a child, and an adult.

1. Fold three index cards in half by placing the long sides together.

2. Draw a baby on the side of one card. Write "Baby" at the bottom of the card as shown.

3. Draw a 1-quart (1-L) jar filled with red liquid.

4. Draw a child on the side of the second card. Write "Child" at the bottom of the card as shown.

5. Draw three 1-quart (1-L) jars filled with red liquid.

6. Draw an adult on the last index card. Write "Adult" at the bottom of the card as shown.

7. Draw five 1-quart (1-L) jars filled with red liquid.

ACTIVITY 2

13

Answer Sheet

How Much

● ● ● ● ● ● ● ● ● ● ● ● ● ● ● ● ● ● ●

Directions: Stand the cards on your worktable or desk. Circle the number that completes each sentence.

1. The body of an adult has about _____ quarts (liters) of blood.

    1   2   3   4   5

2. The body of a child has about _____ quarts (liters) of blood.

    1   2   3   4   5

3. The body of a baby has about _____ quart (liter) of blood.

    1   2   3   4   5

Directions: Write the greater than (>) or less than (<) symbol in the blanks.

4. 3 quarts are _____ 1 quart

5. 3 quarts are _____ 5 quarts

6. 1 liter is _____ 3 liters

7. 5 liters are _____ 1 liter

Directions: Circle the word that completes each sentence.

8. The amount of blood in a child is < the amount of blood in an _____ .

    baby   adult

9. The amount of blood in a child is > the amount of blood in a _____ .

    baby   adult

Weight

Benchmarks

By the end of grade 2, students should be able to
- Measure weight in nonstandard and standard units.
- Recognize and use models that approximate standard units (metric and English) of weight.
- Use standard tools to measure weight.
- Estimate measurements of weight.

In this chapter, students are expected to
- Estimate the weight of different objects.
- Use measuring tools to determine weight measurements.
- Compare the weights of different objects.

Preparing the Materials

Activity 1: Weight
- Make a copy of the Weight activity instruction and answer sheets for each student.

Activity 2: In Order
- Make a copy of the In Order activity sheet for each student.
- Make blue and yellow crayons available for each student.

Investigation 1: Heavy
- Make a copy of the Heavy investigation sheet for each student.
- Students need to work in groups of two or more.
- Make a marker and 10 to 15 coins available for each group of students.
- Caution students about putting things such as coins into their mouth, nose, eyes, ears, and so on.
- Use the following procedure to prepare a rubber band scale for each group.
  (1) Write "TOP" on one of the short sides of a 4-by-12-inch (10-by-30-cm) piece of cardboard.

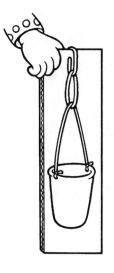

(2) Attach a large paper clip to the center of one of the short sides of the cardboard.
(3) Hang a rubber band on the paper clip.
(4) Use a pencil to punch two holes on opposite sides of a 9-ounce (270-mL) paper cup just under the rim. Note: The cup should be no taller than 4 inches (10 cm).
(5) Loop a 12-inch (30-cm) piece of string through the rubber band and tie the ends through each hole in the cup. The bottom of the cup should be about 1 inch (2.5 cm) above the bottom of the cardboard so that the cup hangs freely when the scale stands on a table.

Presenting the Science Concepts

1. Introduce the new terms:

   ounce (oz)   A standard English unit for weight that is less than a pound. There are 16 ounces in 1 pound.

   pound (lb)   A standard English unit for weight that is less than a ton. There are 2,000 pounds in 1 ton.

   ton (T)   A standard English unit for weight that is bigger than a pound.

   weight   How heavy an object is. How much something is pulled down.

2. Explore the new terms:
   - Weight is a measure of the force of gravity pulling an object down toward the ground.

- The three common English weight units in order from least to greatest are: ounce, pound, and ton.
- One slice of cheese weighs about 1 ounce.
- One loaf of bread weighs about 1 pound.
- One compact car weighs about 1 ton.
- The comparison between English weight units is:

    16 ounces = 1 pound

    2,000 pounds = 1 ton

- Metric weight units include the metric ton (MT) and the newton (N). The metric ton is greater than the English ton. The newton is a smaller unit than the English pound unit.

    1 metric ton = 2,240 pounds

    4.4 newtons = 1 pound

- The metric units of kilogram (kg) and gram (g) are mass units but are often used to indicate the weight of an object.

    1 pound = 2.2 kg

    1 pound = 454 g

- The endings "er" and "est" are added to describing words to form comparative adjectives. For example, smaller and smallest.

EXTENSION

Students can use the rubber band scale and coins from Investigation 1: Heavy to compare the weight of other things to the coins. For example, they can use modeling clay to make a small clay figure of an animal that will fit inside the cup. Then the figure will be weighed and the following questions can be answered.

1. Is the clay figure heavier than 5 coins?
2. Is the clay figure heavier than 10 coins?

ANSWERS

Activity 1: Weight
1. carrot
2. slice of bread
3. baby
4. A

Activity 2: In Order
1. heaviest __3__ heavy __1__ heavier __2__
2. bigger __2__ biggest __3__ big __1__
3. The 10-lb. dog should have been colored yellow

Investigation 1: Heavy
11A. more
  B. less
12A. down
  B. more

Weight

Weight is a measure of how heavy an object is. Standard English units for measuring weight include the **ounce (oz)**, the **pound (lb)**, and the **ton (T)**.

1 pound (lb) = 16 ounces (oz)

1 ton (T) = 2,000 pounds (lb)

Examples:

= 1 ton (T)

= 1 pound (lb)

= 1 ounce (oz)

14 Weight

Directions: Circle the correct answer for each question.

1. Which object weighs less than 1 pound?

2. Which object weighs about 2 ounces?

3. Which object weighs 8 pounds?

4. What is the weight of the elephant?

   A. 2 tons

   B. 2 pounds

   C. 2 ounces

ACTIVITY 2

14 In Order

Directions: Look at each group of pictures. Then write 1, 2, or 3 under the picture to show the order of the comparative adjectives. This first one is done for you.

Example:

long ___1___   longest ___3___   longer ___2___

1. heaviest _____   heavy _____   heavier _____

40 lbs.   60 lbs.   10 lbs.

2. bigger _____   biggest _____   big _____

3. Directions: Color yellow the bulldog that weighs the least.

14 INVESTIGATION 1 **Heavy**

Purpose: To show that weight is how much something is pulled down.

Round Up These Things

1 rubber band scale
1 pen
10 to 15 coins

Things to Do

1. Stand the rubber band scale on a table.

2. Ask a helper to use the pen to make a mark on the cardboard next to the bottom of the rubber band.

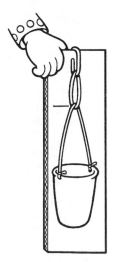

3. Add 5 coins to the cup.

4. Lift the scale.

5. Again, ask a helper to mark the cardboard next to the bottom of the rubber band.

6. While you are holding the scale, ask your helper to add 5 more coins to the cup and to mark the cardboard as before.

7. Remove the coins from the cup. Lay the scale on a table.

8. Write zero next to the first and top mark your helper made.

9. Write 5 next to the second mark.

10. Write 10 next to the third mark.

11. Compare the distance between the lines. Circle the word that completes each data statement.

   A. Ten coins pull the cup down _____ than five coins.

   more   less

   B. Five coins pull the cup down _____ than ten coins.

   more   less

Conclusion:

12. Circle the word that completes each conclusion statement.

   Weight is a measure of how much something is pulled _____.

   A. down   up   sideways

   You can tell that 10 coins have more weight than 5 coins, because the cup with 10 coins is pulled down _____.

   B. more   less   the same

Time

Benchmarks

By the end of grade 2, students should be able to
- Recognize and use models that approximate standard units of time.
- Use standard tools to measure time.
- Estimate time by describing activities that take approximately one second, one minute, and one hour.
- Describe time on a clock using hours, minutes, and seconds.

In this chapter, students are expected to
- Determine time using the hour and minute hands on a clock.

Preparing the Materials

Activity 1: Time—Hour
- Make a copy of the Time—Hour activity sheet for each student.

Activity 2: Minutes—Count by Five
- Make a copy of the Minutes—Count by Five activity sheet for each student.

Activity 3: Time—Seconds
- Make a copy of the Time—Seconds activity sheet for each student.
- Make available a clock or a watch with a second hand for each student or group of students.

Activity 4: Digital Clocks
- Make a copy of the Digital Clocks activity instruction and answer sheets for each student.

Presenting the Science Concepts

1. Introduce the new terms:

   clock   An instrument used to tell time.

   clock face   The part of a clock where the numbers are.

   clock hands   The moving parts on the face of a clock that are used to tell time.

   hour   A standard unit of time that is longer than a minute. There are 60 minutes in 1 hour.

   hour hand   The short clock hand that tells the hour.

   minute   A standard unit of time that is longer than a second. There are 60 seconds in 1 minute.

   minute hand   The long clock hand that tells how many minutes are past the hour.

   second   A standard unit of time that is shorter than a minute.

   second hand   The clock hand that tells how many seconds are past a minute.

2. Explore the new terms:
   - The hands on a clock are identified by their size. The hour and minute hands are the widest, with the hour hand being shorter than the minute hand. The second hand is generally the thinnest and longest hand.
   - The second hand moves faster than the other hands.
   - The hour hand moves the slowest of the three hands.

EXTENSION

- It takes one minute for the second hand to make one complete turn around the clock's face. Because it takes five seconds for the second hand to move from one number to the next, you can count by fives to discover how many seconds are in one minute. Using the clock diagram in Activity 2, students can count by fives as they touch each number. Instruct them to follow the procedure in the activity. Pointing to number 1, say five. Pointing to the number 2, say ten. And so on. This time, instead of counting minutes, they are counting seconds in one minute.

TEACHING TIPS (continued)

• One way to measure time without an instrument is by counting. It takes about one second to say "one thousand and one." Students can investigate this for themselves by measuring how long it takes to count off 10 seconds by saying, "One thousand and one, one thousand and two," and so on.

ANSWERS

Activity 1: Time—Hour

1. 1
2. 12
3. 8
4. 11
5. 10
6. 2
7. 9
8. 3

Activity 2: Minutes—Count by Five

1. 60
2. 60

Activity 3: Time—Seconds

3. 5
4. 5
5. 5 seconds

Activity 4: Digital Clocks

1. 10:00
2. 7:30
3. The hour hand should point to the 12; the minute hand should point to the 2.
4. The hour hand should point to the 5; the minute hand should point to the 3.

ACTIVITY 1

15

Time—Hour

Standard units of time include **hours** and **minutes**. One hour is equal to 60 minutes. **Clocks** are instruments used to tell time. A clock has a **clock face** with numbers and moving parts called **clock hands**. The **hour hand** is shorter than the **minute hand**. The hour hand tells the hour. The minute hand tells how many minutes are after or before the hour. When the minute hand is on the number 12, it is the beginning of the hour.

Directions: Look at the hands of each clock. Write the time.

Example:  ___4___ o'clock

1. _____ o'clock **2.** _____ o'clock **3.** _____ o'clock **4.** _____ o'clock

5. _____ o'clock **6.** _____ o'clock **7.** _____ o'clock **8.** _____ o'clock

ACTIVITY 2

15

Minutes—Count by Five

It takes one hour for the minute hand to make one complete turn around the clock's face. It takes five minutes for the minute hand to move from one number to the next. You can count by fives to discover how many minutes are in one hour.

Directions: Pointing to the face of the clock, count by fives as you touch each number: pointing to the number 1, say five; pointing to the number 2, say ten; and so on. Continue until you touch the number 12.

1. What number do you say when you touch the number 12?

    _____

2. How many minutes are in one hour? _____

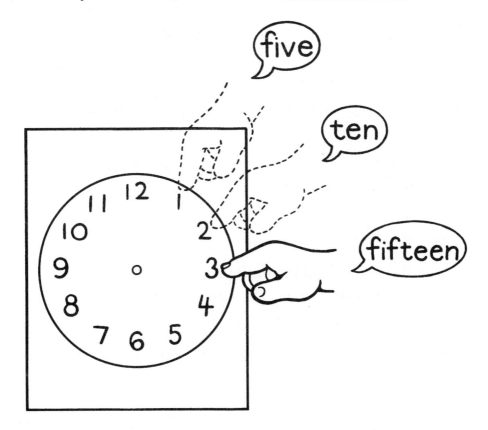

Time—Seconds

A **second** is a unit of time that is shorter than a minute. A **second hand** is the hand on a watch or a clock that tells how many seconds are past a minute. Every time the second hand on a watch or a clock moves, one second of time passes. Starting at number 12, or any number on the clock, the second hand moves five times before reaching the next number. That means it takes five seconds for the second hand to move from one number to the next.

SECOND HAND

Directions: Follow the steps.

1. Look at the clock and find the three hands.

2. Locate the hand that is thinner and moving faster than the other two hands. This is called the **second hand**. It tells the seconds after the minutes.

3. Watch the second hand until it points to a number, such as the number 12. Then count how many times it moves before it points to the next number on the clock, such as the number 1.

   How many times did the second hand move? _____

4. Repeat step 3, with the second hand pointing to another number. Count the seconds before the hand reaches the next number.

   How many times did the second hand move? _____

5. How many seconds does it take for the second hand to move from one number to the next? _____

© 2007 by John Wiley & Sons, Inc.

Digital Clocks

Digital clocks do not have hands. Instead, they have numbers that show the time in hours and minutes. The number of the hour comes before the colon symbol (:) and the number of minutes after the hour comes after the colon symbol.

Examples:

ACTIVITY 4

15

Instruction Sheet

Digital Clocks

● ●

Directions: Look at each clock. Then write the same time on the digital clock.

1.

2.

Directions: Look at the digital clock. Then draw the hands on the clock to show the same time.

3.

4.

Temperature

Benchmarks

By the end of grade 2, students should be able to
- Recognize and use models that approximate standard units (metric and English) of temperature.
- Explain and record observations using pictures and objects.
- Demonstrate how temperature is measured using models that approximate standard units.
- Use standard tools to measure temperature.

In this chapter, students are expected to
- Distinguish between things that are hot and cold.
- Read models of Fahrenheit and Celsius thermometers.
- Use models of Fahrenheit and Celsius thermometers.

Preparing the Materials

Activity 1: Hot or Cold
- Make a copy of the Hot or Cold activity sheet for each student or group.

Activity 2: Fahrenheit Thermometer
- Make a copy of the Fahrenheit Thermometer activity instruction and answer sheets for each student.
- Make crayons available for each student.

Activity 3: Celsius Thermometer
- Make a copy of the Celsius Thermometer activity instruction and answer sheets for each student.
- Make crayons available for each student.

Activity 4: Model Thermometer—Fahrenheit
- Make a copy of the Model Thermometer—Fahrenheit activity sheet for each student.
- Use the Fahrenheit thermometer pattern on page 167 to make a Fahrenheit model thermometer available for each student. Make the models using these steps:

1. Color the liquid strip and bulb portion of the thermometer pattern red.
2. Laminate the colored patterns. (This is an optional step.)
3. Cut out the two indicated areas.
4. Cut along the dotted line to separate the liquid strip from the other sections.
5. Score each fold line by laying a ruler along each of the fold lines, then trace the lines with a pen.
6. Fold the paper along "fold line 1," then along "fold line 2," and secure the folded sections together with tape.
7. Insert the liquid strip in the liquid strip slot so that the colored side of the strip is visible through the openings in the front of the model.

- Make a red crayon available for each student.

Activity 5: Model Thermometer—Celsius
- Make a copy of the Model Thermometer—Celsius activity sheet for each student.
- Use the Celsius thermometer pattern on page 168 to make a Celsius model thermometer available for each student. (See instructions above.)
- Make a red crayon available for each student.

Investigation 1: Up and Down
- Make a copy of the Up and Down investigation instruction and answer sheets for each student.
- Make available a thermometer, a red crayon, and a wet cotton ball for each student or group.

Presenting the Science Concepts

1. Introduce the new terms:

   degree (°)   The unit of measuring temperature.

   degree Celsius (°C)   A unit of measuring temperature on a Celsius thermometer.

   degree Fahrenheit (°F)   A unit of measuring temperature on a Fahrenheit thermometer.

. . . .

temperature A measurement of how cold or hot something is.

2. Explore the new terms:

- Celsius is a metric unit of measuring temperature on a Celsius thermometer.

- Fahrenheit is an English unit of measuring temperature on a Fahrenheit thermometer.

- Two common thermometers are Celsius and Fahrenheit. The scales on these two thermometers are not the same. For example, the freezing and boiling temperatures of water on a Celsius thermometer are 0°C and 100°C. On the Fahrenheit thermometer the freezing and boiling temperatures of water are 32°F and 212°F.

- Fahrenheit scales generally have five divisions between each printed number. Each division equals 2°.

- Celsius scales generally have 10 divisions between each printed number. Each division equals 1°.

EXTENSION

Use the Fahrenheit and Celsius thermometer models to evaluate a student's ability to read both the Fahrenheit and Celsius thermometer scales.

ANSWERS

Activity 1: Hot or Cold

1. cold
2. hot

Activity 2: Fahrenheit Thermometer

1. 48°F
2. 106°F
3. Thermometer should be colored up to the third mark above 30°F.
4. Thermometer should be colored up to the fourth mark above 60°F.

Activity 3: Celsius Thermometer

1. 34°C
2. 104°C
3. Thermometer should be colored up to the second mark above 30°C.
4. Thermometer should be colored up to the seventh mark above 70°C.

Activity 4: Model Thermometer–Fahrenheit

1. 46°F
2. 54°F
3. 32°F

Activity 5: Model Thermometer–Celsius

1. 15°C
2. 28°C
3. 0°C

Investigation 1: Up and Down

1. highest
2. lowest
3. highest
4. lowest

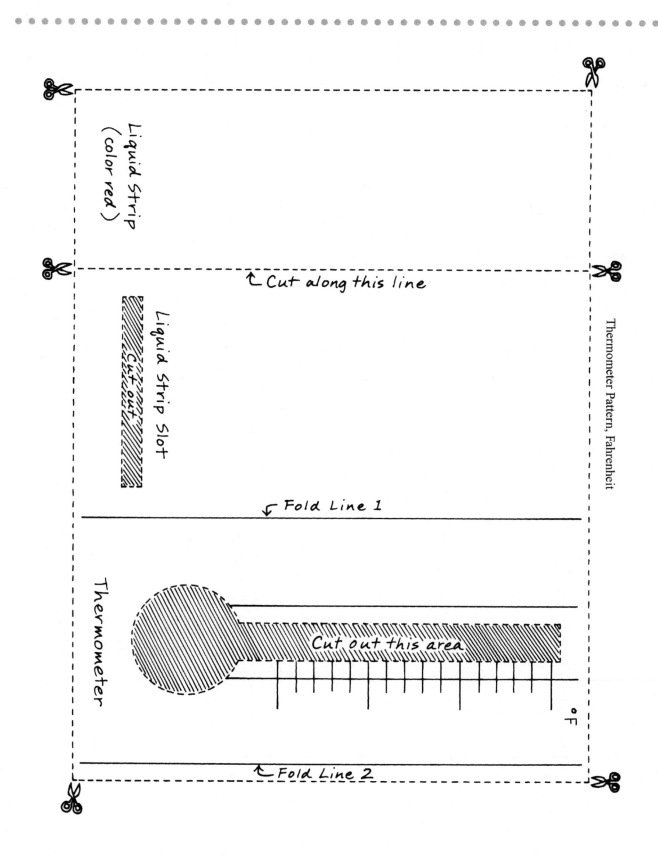

Liquid Strip
(color red)

Cut along this line

Liquid Strip Slot

Cut out

Fold Line 1

Thermometer

Cut out this area

°F

Fold Line 2

Thermometer Pattern, Fahrenheit

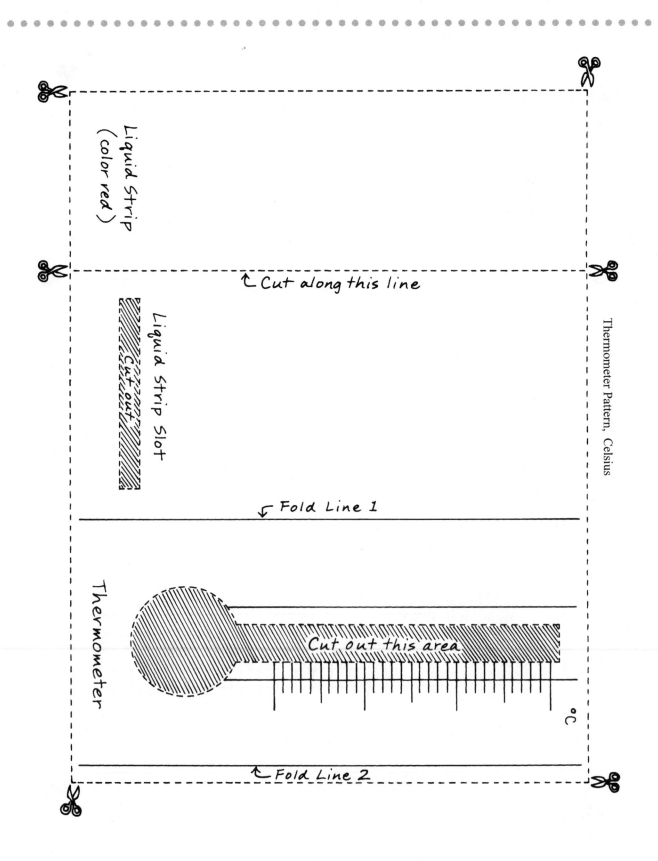

Liquid Strip
(color red)

Cut along this line

Liquid Strip Slot

Cut out

Fold Line 1

Thermometer

Cut out this area

°C

Fold Line 2

Thermometer Pattern, Celsius

ACTIVITY 1

16

Hot or Cold

Temperature is a measurement of how cold or hot something is.

Directions: Look at each picture. Then write *hot* or *cold* beneath each picture to tell if the outdoor temperature in the picture is hot or cold.

1. _____

2. _____

Fahrenheit Thermometer

A thermometer is an instrument that measures temperature in a unit called a **degree** (°). A Fahrenheit thermometer measures in **degrees Fahrenheit, °F**.

Directions: Read the Fahrenheit thermometer and record the temperature in degrees Fahrenheit, °F. This example is done for you.

Example:

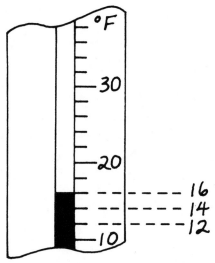

- There are 10° between each numbered mark.

- There are 4 unnumbered marks between each numbered mark.

- Each unnumbered mark is equal to 2°F.

- The height of the liquid in the thermometer is at the third unnumbered mark above 10°F.

- Start with the number 10 mark, then count up by twos. The third unnumbered mark would be: 10, 12, 14, **16**.

Answer: _____ 16°F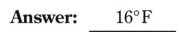

Example:

Directions: Color in the thermometer so that it shows the indicated temperature. This example is done for you.

- The height of the liquid in the thermometer should be at the first unnumbered mark above 20°F.

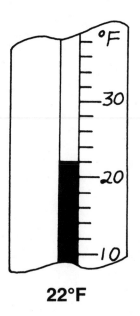

22°F

ACTIVITY 2
16
Answer Sheet

Fahrenheit Thermometer

● ●

Directions: Read the Fahrenheit thermometer and record the temperature in degrees Fahrenheit, F°.

1. _____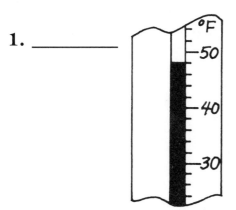

2. _____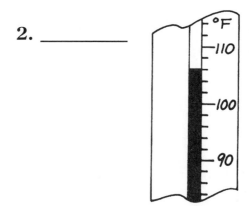

Directions: Color in the thermometers so that each shows the indicated temperature.

3.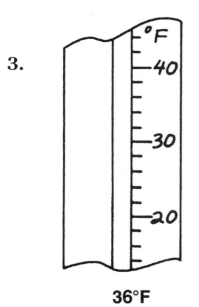

36°F

4.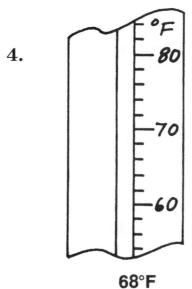

68°F

Celsius Thermometer

The **Celsius thermometer** is a type of standard thermometer. A Celsius thermometer measures in **degrees Celsius, °C.**

Directions: Read the Celsius thermometer and record the temperature in degrees Celsius, °C. This example is done for you.

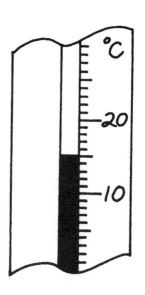

Example:

- There are 10° between each numbered mark.

- There are 9 unnumbered marks between each numbered mark.

- Each unnumbered mark is equal to 1°C.

- The height of the liquid in the thermometer is at the fifth unnumbered mark above 10°C.

- Start with the number 10 mark, then count by ones until you reach the fifth unnumbered mark: 11, 12, 13, 14, **15.**

Answer: _____15°C_____

Example:

Directions: Color in the thermometer so that it shows the indicated temperature. This example is done for you.

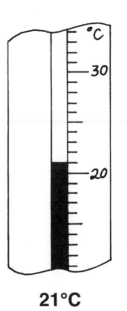

- The height of the liquid in the thermometer should be at the first unnumbered mark above 20°C.

21°C

Celsius Thermometer

● ● ● ● ● ● ● ● ● ● ● ● ● ● ● ● ● ●

Directions: Read the Celsius thermometer and record the temperature in degrees Celsius, C°.

1. _____

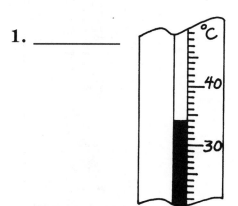

2. _____

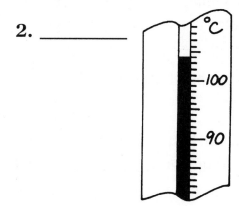

Directions: Color in the thermometers so that each shows the indicated temperature.

3.

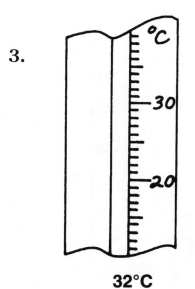

32°C

4.

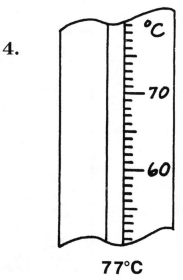

77°C

ACTIVITY 4
16
Model Thermometer—Fahrenheit

Directions:

1. Color the sliding strips in each of the figures.

2. Move the sliding liquid strip in the model thermometer to match the position of the strip in the figure.

3. Write the temperature in the blank.

Example:

- On a Fahrenheit thermometer scale, the difference between unnumbered marks equals 2°F.

- The top of the liquid strip is even with the first mark above 50°F.

Temperature: ___52°F___

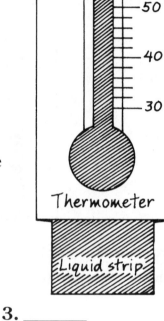

Thermometer

Liquid strip

1. _____

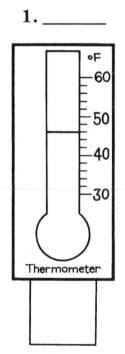

Thermometer

2. _____

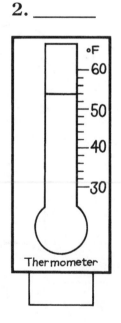

Thermometer

3. _____

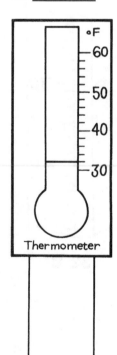

Thermometer

Model Thermometer— Celsius

ACTIVITY 5

16

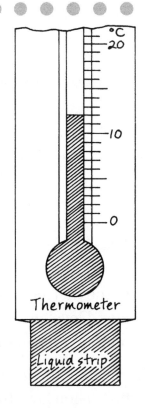

Thermometer

Liquid strip

Directions:

1. Color the sliding strips in each of the figures.

2. Move the sliding liquid strip in the model thermometer to match the position of the strip in the figure.

3. Write the temperature in the blank.

Example:

• On a Celsius scale, the difference between unnumbered marks equals 1°C.

• The top of the liquid strip is even with the second mark above 10°C.

Temperature: ___12°C___

1. _____

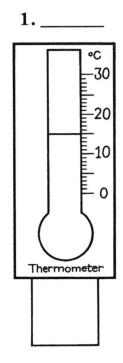

Thermometer

2. _____

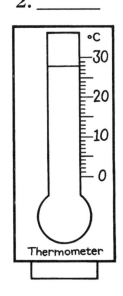

Thermometer

3. _____

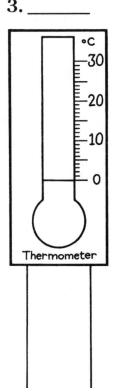

Thermometer

Up and Down

Round Up These Things

1 thermometer
1 red crayon
1 wet cotton ball

Things to Do

1. Place the thermometer on a table. Observe the level of the liquid line in the thermometer. Color this liquid level in "Thermometer A" on the Temperature Data chart.

2. Separate the fibers of the cotton ball. Then lay a thin layer of wet cotton across the bulb of the thermometer.

3. Keeping your mouth about 4 inches (10 cm) away from the wet cotton, blow your breath across the wet cotton about 15 times.

4. Observe the level of the liquid line in the thermometer again. Color this liquid level in "Thermometer B" on the Temperature Data chart.

Up and Down

●●●●●●●●●●●●●●●●●●●●●●●

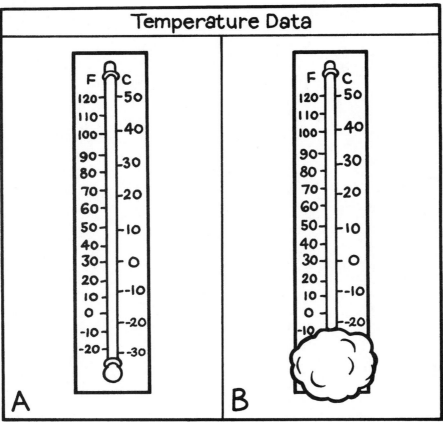

Temperature Data

A   B

Directions: Circle the word that completes each sentence.

1. Thermometer A has the _____ liquid level.

    lowest   highest

2. Thermometer B has the _____ liquid level.

    lowest   highest

3. Thermometer A has the _____ temperature.

    lowest   highest

4. Thermometer B has the _____ temperature.

    lowest   highest

Grouping

Grouping is the act of putting things together. *Classifying* is to group things by their properties. *Sequencing* is to group things in order, such as by number order, ABC order, or order in time. An understanding of grouping helps kids to design scientific investigations and to organize the results.

Classifying

Benchmarks

By the end of grade 2, students should be able to
- Classify things by properties.
- Use pictures to make generalizations about combining things.

In this chapter, students are expected to
- Use tree diagrams to find all possible groupings of things.
- Identify living and nonliving things.
- Identify groups of similar things.
- Make leaf rubbings.
- Classify leaves by vein types.

Preparing the Materials

Activity 1: Classify—Living or Nonliving
- Make a copy of the Classify—Living or Nonliving activity sheet for each student.

Activity 2: Classify—These Don't Belong
- Make a copy of the Classify—These Don't Belong activity sheet for each student.
- Make crayons or markers available for each student.

Activity 3: Tree Diagram
- Make a copy of the Tree Diagram activity instruction and answer sheets for each student.

Activity 4: Classify—Leaves
- Make a copy of the Classify—Leaves activity sheet for each student.
- Make crayons available for each student.

Investigation 1: Rubbings
- Make a copy of the Rubbings investigation instruction sheet for each student.
- Make available leaves with the two types of vein patterns—parallel and netted. Each student needs four leaves.
- Cut 1 sheet of white copy paper into four parts for each student.
- Make crayons and newspaper available for each student.

Presenting the Science Concepts

1. Introduce the new terms:

    classify   To group or sort things by their properties.

    tree diagram   A branching diagram that shows all possible groupings of things.

2. Explore the new terms:
    - Different properties can be used to classify the same things. For example, things can be classified by whether they are living or nonliving. The same things can be classified by color, shape, size, or texture.
    - A tree diagram looks like the branches of a tree. The structure of the tree shows all the possible groupings of things being classified.
    - When making leaf rubbings, more of the crayon is rubbed off by the rough edges of the leaves as well as the veins in the leaves. So a leaf rubbing is a print of the leaf.

EXTENSION

A homework assignment for students might be to collect leaf rubbings in their neighborhood or a nearby park with adult assistance. The rubbings can be studied by the class and grouped in different ways, such as by vein type or edge type (smooth or rough).

ANSWERS

Activity 1: Classify–Living or Nonliving

These parts of the pictures should be colored.

A. dog

B. cactus

C. fish

D. parrot

TEACHING TIPS (continued)

Activity 2: Classify—These Don't Belong

1. **Row 1** circle the snake
   Row 2 circle the octopus

2. **Row 1** snake
   Row 2 nonliving

Activity 3: Tree Diagram

1. Bill
2. Kim
3. Harry
4. Rob

Activity 4: Classify—Leaves

1. Students should draw parallel veins in the blades of grass.

2. Students should draw netted veins in the sweetgum leaf.

Investigation 1: Rubbings

Students should label their leaf rubbings as parallel veins or netted veins.

ACTIVITY 1

17 Classify—Living or Nonliving

Classifying means to group things by their properties. Living things include people, animals, and plants. Nonliving things include rocks, furniture, clothes, and dishes.

Directions: Color only the living parts of each picture.

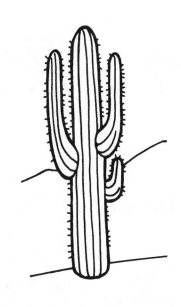

ACTIVITY 2

17

Classify—These Don't Belong

NAME _____

1. Directions: Color the one picture in each row that does not belong in the group.

Row 1   Kinds of Animals

Row 2   Living Things

2. Directions: Circle the word that completes the sentence.

Row 1   What doesn't belong is a _____.

           bug   snake

Row 2   What doesn't belong is _____.

           nonliving   living

Tree Diagram

A **tree diagram** is a branching diagram that shows all possible groupings of things.

See the example of using a tree diagram below.

Directions: Read the story. Then follow the instructions.

Mrs. Bolden is planning an outdoor science investigation for her class. The class will be in two groups. Each group will wear a different color hat. She has red and blue hats in three sizes—small, medium, and large. To help students pick out the right color and size, Mrs. Bolden groups the hats by color and size.

Study Mrs. Bolden's hat tree diagram. How many different groups of hats are there?

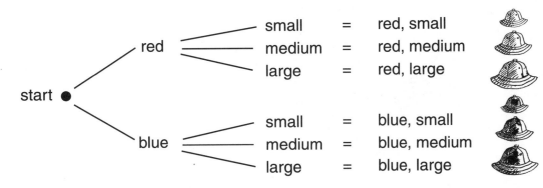

- At the start, all the hats are in one group.

- Next, the hats are divided into two groups: a red group and a blue group.

- Last, each color group is divided into three sizes: small, medium, and large

- There are three groups of red hats and three groups of blue hats.

Answer: ___6 groups of hats___

NAME _____

Tree Diagram

• • • • • • • • • • • • • • • • • • •

Directions: Read the story. Then follow the instructions.

Davin is researching hair. He wants to group the information by hair type. He has chosen two colors (blond and brunette) and two styles (curly and straight).

Study Davin's hair tree diagram. Match a person to each group. Write the name of the person in the blank space.

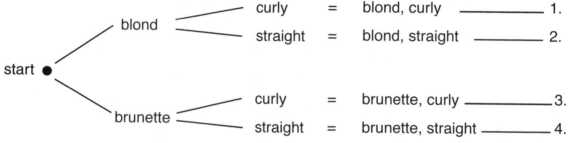

start ●

blond
— curly   =   blond, curly   _____ 1.
— straight =   blond, straight _____ 2.

brunette
— curly   =   brunette, curly _____ 3.
— straight =   brunette, straight _____ 4.

Harry

Bill

Rob

Kim

ACTIVITY 4

17

Classify—Leaves

Veins in leaves are the tubelike structures that carry food to the plant. The two types of vein patterns are parallel and netted. **Parallel veins** form a pattern of veins that go in the same direction. **Netted veins** form a pattern of veins that branch out in many different directions.

Lily

Maple

Directions: Read about each leaf. Then draw the veins.

1. Grass is an example of a leaf with parallel veins.

Grass

2. The netted veins in a sweetgum leaf start at the stem of the leaves and branch out.

Sweetgum

Rubbings

Purpose: To learn how to make rubbings.

Round Up These Things

1 piece of newspaper
leaves
4 pieces of white paper
crayons

Things to Do

1. Place the newspaper on a table to protect the table's surface.

2. Lay one of the leaves on the newspaper with the rough side of the leaf facing up.

3. Cover the leaf with one of the pieces of white paper.

4. With firm pressure, rub a crayon across the paper over the leaf until a colored print of the leaf is made.

5. Repeat steps 2 through 4 using the remaining leaves and papers.

6. Label your leaf rubbings as parallel veins or netted veins.

Sequencing

Benchmarks

By the end of grade 2, students should be able to
- Use patterns to make predictions.
- Describe order of events.
- List things in order using numbers.
- Identify the numerical order of directions.

In this chapter, students are expected to
- Match directions with describing figures.
- Use language such as "before" or "after" to describe relative position in a sequence of events.

Preparing the Materials

Activity 1: Sequencing—Putting Steps in Order
- Make a copy of the Sequencing—Putting Steps in Order activity sheet for each student.

Activity 2: Sequencing—Morning Glories
- Make a copy of the Sequencing—Morning Glories activity instruction and answer sheets for each student.
- Make as many copies of the flower pattern on page 190 as necessary so that each student has a paper flower. Cut out the flower patterns.
- Make a newspaper flower for each student using these steps:
  1. Stack five sheets of newspaper. Lay one of the flower patterns on the top sheet, and trace around the pattern.
  2. Cutting through all layers of newspaper, cut out the tracing.
  3. Repeat the steps to make more newspaper flowers.
- For very young students, crease the fold lines on the newspaper flower using the procedure in the student investigation.
- For each group of students, prepare a large bowl or plastic container with about 1 inch (2.5 cm) of tap water in it.
- It is very important that the paper flowers stay dry while folding them. Water will cause the petals to stick together and not open. You may wish to have the water container in an area separate from the folding area.
- Students should remove their wet flower after it opens. This prevents flowers from landing on top of one another.
- Make a container available where students may throw out their wet flowers.
- Have paper towels handy for drying hands and spills.

Presenting the Science Concepts

1. Introduce the new terms:

   camouflage   A way of hiding by blending in with the background.

   sequencing   Putting things in order.

   walking stick   An insect that looks like a small stick with branches.

2. Explore the new terms:
   - Sequencing can be in number order, ABC order, or chronological (time) order. An example of chronological order is the growth of a seed to a plant.

EXTENSION

Students can determine if the sequence of petals opening is the same as the sequence in which they were folded. Or is it the reverse order? Or is it some other order? Petals can be folded in different orders. To determine the order of opening, the petals should be numbered with a pencil as they are folded.

ANSWERS

Activity 1: Sequencing–Putting Steps in Order

1. C   3. B
2. D   4. A

Activity 2: Sequencing–Morning Glories

1. A

2 and 3.   Student answers will vary.

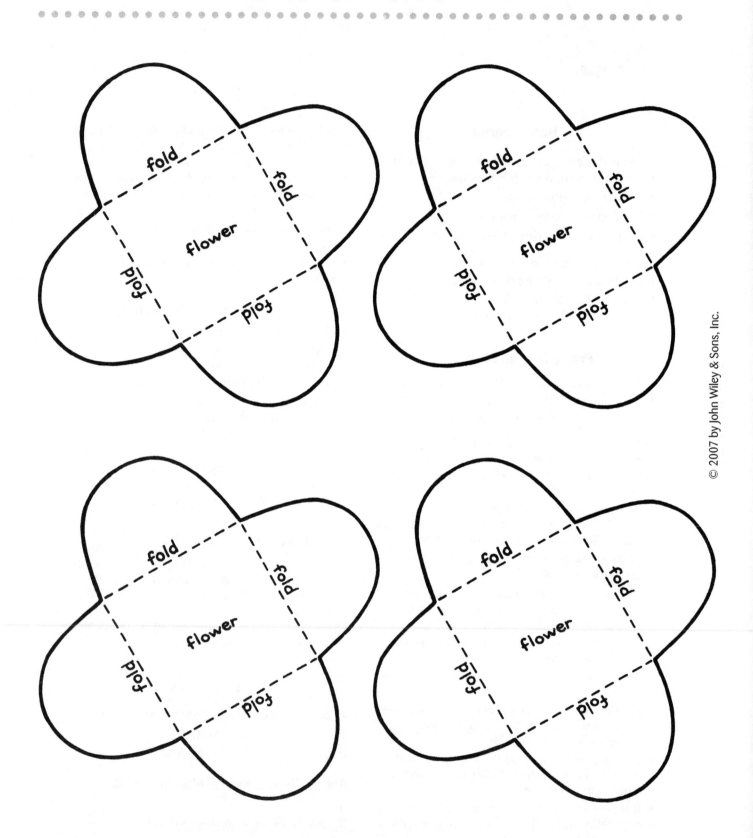

Sequencing—Putting Steps in Order

Sequencing is the order in which things happen. **Camouflage** is a way of hiding by blending in with the background. A **walking stick** is an insect that looks like a small stick with branches. A brown walking stick standing on a brown stick is camouflaged.

Directions: Read the steps for making branches and a walking stick. Write the letter of the picture that goes with each step.

1. Put clay in the bottom of a cup. _____

2. Make branches by twisting together pieces of brown chenille craft stems. Stick the branches into the clay. _____

3. Twist together pieces of brown chenille craft stems to make a walking stick. _____

4. Place the walking stick on the branches. It is hard to tell the walking stick from the branches. _____

A

B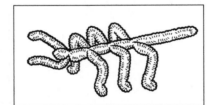

C

D

Sequencing— Morning Glories

Some flowers, such as morning glories, open every morning and close again at night. This occurs because things happen inside the plant, flower, and petals. The sequence for a morning glory to open is:

1. **Sap**, a watery plant food, moves through special tubes in the plant to the flower.

2. As the flower petals fill with sap, the flower opens.

Directions: Follow the steps in order to make a paper morning glory.

1. Fold one flower petal toward the middle of the flower.

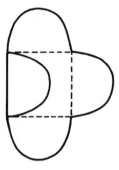

2. Fold a second petal toward the middle of the flower.

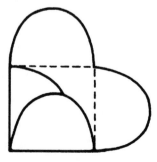

3. Fold a third petal toward the middle of the flower.

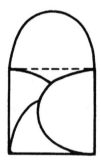

4. Fold the last petal toward the middle of the flower.

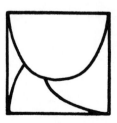

© 2007 by John Wiley & Sons, Inc.

ACTIVITY 2
18
Answer Sheet

Sequencing–
Morning Glories

● ● ● ● ● ● ● ● ● ● ● ● ● ● ● ● ● ●

1. Hold a folded paper morning glory, petal side up, about 4 inches (10 cm) above the water.

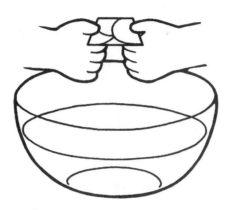

2. Drop the paper into the water.

Directions: Read the sentence. Then circle the letter in front of the sentence of the best answer.

1. What happened when the paper morning glory touched the water?

   A. The petals opened one at a time as they filled with water.

   B. The petals do not open, but the paper gets wet.

2. If a newspaper morning glory was used, predict what will happen.

   A. The petals would open as before.

   B. The petals would open more slowly.

   C. The petals would open faster.

Directions: Repeat the activity using a folded newspaper morning glory. Then write your answer for the question in the blank.

3. Was your prediction correct? _____

Glossary

● ●

ABC order   A word list in order of the alphabet. Also known as alphabetical order.

adjective   A word that describes something.

alligator   An animal with a long scaly body and tail, and a huge mouth with big teeth.

baby   A very young child.

bandage   A covering for a wound.

bark   The sound a dog makes.

bean   A type of seed.

bee   An insect that stings.

bird   An animal that has feathers.

bite   To cut into food with your teeth.

blood   The liquid that carries oxygen and other **nutrients** to all parts of the body.

bones   The hard body parts that hold the body upright.

boy   A young male person.

brain   The part of your body that receives and decodes **nerve** messages so you know how things feel. It is located in your head.

bulldog   A dog with a wrinkled face.

camouflage   A way of hiding by blending in with the background.

capacity   How much something will hold.

caterpillar   A wormlike critter that turns into a butterfly.

cause   An action or an act that makes something happen.

centimeter (cm)   A metric unit of distance. There are 100 centimeters in 1 meter.

chameleon   An animal that can change colors.

chart   A way to organize **data** for viewing.

chest   The part of your body between your neck and belly.

chrysalis   A special sac that a **caterpillar** forms around its body.

classify   To group or sort things by their properties.

clock   An instrument used to tell time.

clock face   The part of a clock where the numbers are.

clock hands   The moving parts on the **face** of a **clock** that are used to tell time.

communication   To pass on information.

conclusion   (1) A summary of information collected including **research** and **experiment results**. (2) Compares a hypothesis with experiment results.

control   A test that other tests are compared to.

controlled variable   A **variable** that is kept the same.

cup (c)   A standard unit of measuring capacity. There are 4 cups in 1 quart.

data   Collected and recorded information.

decibel (dB)   The unit used to measure the loudness of sound.

definition   A statement explaining the meaning of a word.

degree (°)   The unit of measuring **temperature**.

degree Celsius (°C)   A standard unit of measuring **temperature**.

degree Fahrenheit (°F)   A standard unit of measuring **temperature**.

dictionary   A book that contains words in **ABC order** with their definitions.

effect   Something that happens because of a cause.

estimate   A guess about the amount of something without measuring it.

evaporation   The change of a liquid into a gas.

exoskeleton   The outer covering of an insect.

experiment   A test done to answer a problem; an example of a **cause** and an **effect**; a test to check the correctness of a **hypothesis**.

fact   Something that is true.

fingerprint   The ridges on your fingertip that make up a special design.

fish   An animal that has scales and fins, and lives in water.

fist   A hand that is tightly closed.

flavor   How things taste.

flea   An insect that **bites** other animals and makes them itch.

flower   The part of a plant where seeds are made.

foot (ft)   An English unit of distance that is shorter than a **yard (yd)**. There are 3 feet in 1 yard.

frog   An animal that can hop long distances.

gallon (gal)   A standard unit of measuring capacity that is larger than a **quart (qt)**. There are 4 quarts in 1 gallon.

glossary   A short list of definitions in **ABC order** at the back of a book.

graph   A **chart** that compares two sets of data.

gravity   A force that pulls things down.

hearing   One of your **senses**. You hear with your ears.

heart   The body part that pumps **blood**.

height   The measure of the distance from the top to bottom of something that is standing upright.

horse   An animal that can be ridden.

hour   A standard unit of time that is longer than a **minute**. There are 60 minutes in 1 hour.

hour hand   The short clock hand that tells the hour.

hypothesis   An idea that identifies the **effect** because of a **cause**; an idea about what the answer to a problem is.

inch (in)   An English unit of distance that is shorter than a **foot (ft)**. There are 12 inches in 1 foot.

inference   A guess about something based on what you already know.

input variable   A variable that you change.

interpret   Using **data** to explain something or to answer a question.

investigation   The process involved in asking and answering questions.

kilometer (km)   A standard metric unit of distance that is longer than a **meter (m)**. There are 1,000 meters in 1 kilometer.

length   The measure of the distance between two points. The measure of the longest side of an object; equal to or longer than the **width**.

liter (L)   A standard metric unit of measuring capacity.

measure   To find the amount of something.

meter (m)   A metric unit of distance that is longer than a **centimeter (cm)**. There are 100 centimeters in 1 meter.

milliliter (mL) A standard metric unit of measuring capacity that is smaller than a **liter (L)**. There are 1,000 milliliters in 1 liter.

minute A standard unit of time that is longer than a **second**. There are 60 seconds in 1 minute.

minute hand The long clock hand that tells how many **minutes** are past the **hour**.

model (1) Something that is made to represent an object or a thing. (2) To **communicate** information by acting it out.

monkey An animal with a very long tail that can climb trees.

nectar A sweet liquid in flowers.

netted veins A pattern of leaf **veins** that branch out in many different directions.

nerve A tiny threadlike fiber that sends coded messages to your **brain**.

nonstandard unit of measurement Unit of measurement that is not commonly used.

nose The part of the body that identifies **smells**.

nutrients Substances that living organisms need for life and growth.

observing The act of examining something by using your **senses**.

octopus An animal that lives in water and has many arms.

odor Also called **smell** or **scent**.

opinion A belief that someone has about something.

ordinal number A number used to tell the order in a series or a group.

ounce (oz) A standard English unit for **weight** that is less than a **pound (lb)**. There are 16 ounces in 1 pound.

outer ear The part of the ear you can see that collects sounds and directs them inside the ear.

output variable A **variable** that changes because of the **input variable**.

panting Breathing quickly with the mouth open.

parallel veins A pattern of leaf **veins** that go in the same direction.

parrot An animal that can fly and learn to talk.

picture dictionary A **dictionary** with **definitions** and pictures to explain the meaning of a word.

pitch How high or low a **sound** is.

pound (lb) A standard English unit for **weight** that is less than a **ton**. There are 2,000 pounds in 1 ton.

predator An animal that hunts other animals for food.

predict To guess what you think will happen next.

pressure A **touch sense** that lets you know that something is pushing on your body.

prey An animal that is food for a **predator**.

problem A science question to be answered.

proboscis A butterfly's long feeding tube.

procedure The instructional steps of an **experiment**.

pupil The dark spot in the center of your eye.

purpose The goal of an **investigation**.

quart (qt) A standard unit of measuring **capacity** that is smaller than a **gallon (gal)**. There are 4 quarts in 1 gallon.

rabbit An animal with very long ears.

research The process of collecting information about a topic being studied.

results A summary of the data from an **investigation**.

riddle A puzzle made of words that form a question that needs an answer.

ruler   An instrument used to measure distance.

saliva   The liquid in your mouth that softens food.

sap   A watery plant food that moves through special tubes in a plant.

scent   A certain **smell**.

scientific method   The steps of an investigation used in asking and answering a science question.

second   A standard unit of time that is shorter than a **minute**.

second hand   The clock hand that tells how many seconds are past a minute.

seed coat   The covering on the outside of a bean.

seed food   The part of the inside of a bean where food is stored.

seed plant   A structure inside a bean that looks like a baby plant.

senses   What an organism uses to know and feel what is going on around it.

sequencing   Putting things in order.

sight   One of your **senses**. You need your eyes to see.

skin   The outer protective covering on your body.

smell   A **sense** that identifies **scents**; the scent itself.

sound   Energy produced by **vibrating** objects.

spider   An animal with eight legs that spins a web.

standard unit of measurement   Unit found on a measuring tool.

symbol   Something that stands for or represents something else.

table   A type of **chart** with columns and rows.

tablespoon (tbs)   A standard unit of measuring **capacity** that is larger than a **teaspoon (tsp)**. There are 3 teaspoons in 1 tablespoon.

taste   One of your **senses**. You need **taste buds** to taste.

taste buds   Groups of cells on your **tongue** that let you taste things that are sweet, salty, bitter, and sour.

teaspoon (tsp)   A standard unit of measuring **capacity** that is smaller than a **tablespoon (T)**. There are 3 teaspoons in 1 tablespoon.

temperature   A measurement of how cold or hot something is.

thermometer   An instrument that **measures temperature**.

thorax   The part of an insect's body to which its wings and legs are attached.

ton (t)   A standard English unit for **weight** that is more than a **pound**.

tongue   The part of the body used for tasting.

touch   One of the body's five **senses**.

tree diagram   A branching diagram that shows all possible groupings of things.

variable   Something that can be changed or can change on its own.

veins   The tubelike structures in leaves that carry food to the plant.

vibrate   To shake or move back and forth.

vocal cords   Two small rubber band–like flaps in your throat that vibrate when air from the lungs passes through them.

walking stick   An insect that looks like a small stick with branches.

weight   How heavy an object is. How much something is pulled down.

whiskers   Hairs that grow on an animal's face.

width   The **measure** of distance from one side to the other of something. The **measure** of the distance from side to side of an object; equal to or shorter than the **length**.

yard (yd)   An English unit of distance that is longer than a **foot (ft)**. There are 3 feet in 1 yard.

Index